Growing Confident

10 Steps To A More Confident You

Jorge Vence

First Edition 2015

DragonRising Publishing
United Kingdom

ISBN 978-1-908269-62-1

Published By
DragonRising Publishing
United Kingdom
www.DragonRising.com

Table of Contents

Acknowledgements

First and foremost I would like to thank God for having given me a second chance when I thought my life had ended.

A thank you that goes beyond words to my mother, Carmen Gonzalez, for she gave me life, not once but twice. I do not know what would have happened if my mother hadn't woken me up when I turned my back on life.

To my brother, Luis Enrique Vence. He held the mirror I needed to see my reflection in to wake up and break away from unwanted behaviours and beliefs. From the bottom of my heart, thank you.

A huge thank you goes to Donal Hogan. Without you I do not know where I would be today! You have been a great part of my success and I will be forever thankful you believed in me more than I ever believed in myself. Who would have thought that that young man you met once would be a confident man today?

I want to thank all my clients and friends. You are my teachers and inspiration. There are too many of you to even begin. You know who you are though. I love you all.

A special heartfelt and warm thank you goes to all my EFT peers, my NLP Master Practitioners, NLP Trainers. To all the incredible trainers who saw much more potential in me than I ever fathomed - thank you, thank you, thank you... You were all part of my growth as a Confident man.

Thank you to Tracey Middleton for having taken the time from your busy schedule to help me edit my first manuscript.

I want to thank the people I saw in the streets while I was typing these pages. You brought many ideas to my conscious awareness during the process.

No project would ever be completed without cheerleaders, people you meet and who make you feel so good when you are around them. At the same time they praise you and motivate you when you need it the most (without them even knowing it!). Two beautiful women come to mind, Rebecca Green and Sharon Bowler. You bring joy, hope and love into my life when I am around you.

A thank you to all my teachers and mentors from the past, those with whom I learned valuable lessons about life and myself. Without you I would have not learned half the things I know nowadays.

I want to thank you, the reader, for believing this book will touch and transform your life. You are the real reason this book has seen the light. You are the reason I Grew Confident. Thank you for being a fighter and a believer, thank you for believing in yourself.

I would like to thank the plants and animals of the planet. They are the reason we are alive and they don't expect anything in return - I honour them. Thank you for the air and the food I get every day.

Silvia Hartmann, what can I say? Words will never suffice to thank you for your kindness, your abundance, for paving the way for me and many others and for being a real pioneer in Modern Energism.

Silvia, thank you for encouraging me to put pen to paper or, in this case, fingers to keyboard. Before meeting you I was doubtful about my skills and capability of sharing my story with the world. Because of you, I now know I can and I will continue to do so.

Everyone at the GOE, you are an incredible group of people - friendly, caring and you simply make anyone's day sweeter when they come into contact with you.

To Anastasio Yap, I may not have seen you in many years but in my heart you live. It is ironic to think you are that link that joins my past and my present. Had I not followed your advice, I honestly could not say whether I would be where I am right now. Thank you, I love you.

To my biology teacher, Judith Atencio, from high school, you heard me when my voice was faint and weak. You gave me three beautiful gifts I will never forget: Einstein the cat – when I had no one to keep me company; you gave me love for knowledge and science; and, most importantly, you gave me guidance, love and support when I almost lost faith in humanity.

Lastly, but certainly not least, to my friend, lover, accomplice, inspiration, rock, the wind beneath my wings – Martin MacKenzie, you are the real reason I have Grown Confident. When I met you I was at a crossroads.

I was at a point in my life when a decision had to be made. With your presence, love and support I knew what road to follow and what to do.

You have been there for me when I doubted myself, when I felt trapped and not knowing what to do. You made my transition into this wonderful life I now experience easier and effortless. I wish I could put into words how much I love you and how much I value everything you do, have done and continue to do for me. You have the patience of an angel. During this process you stood back and, rather than demand my attention, you supported me every step of the way, because you knew what this meant to me, possibly even more than I did at the time.

You know the real me and at the same time you have witnessed my journey to where I am. At times you have taken a back seat and let me get on with what I had to do. If that isn't love, I do not know what else could prove it more than that.

You have always been there for me and this is to you, thank you! You really are the reason I am the person I am today. Together we both Grew Confident because of your integrity, solidarity and charisma. What would life be like without you? I do not know nor do I wish to find out. One thing is for certain, this book would not be here if you hadn't been in my life. I love you to the moon and back, to infinity and beyond and back.

Thank you, thank you, thank you...

Jorge

Foreword By Silvia Hartmann

In this wonderfully inspiring book, author, trainer and poet Jorge Vence shares his insights and his journey of discovery of how to become a confident person, someone who is in charge of their life and has the energy to go out there to make the world a better place.

For many decades, the New Age school of personal development has held that you are perfect just the way you are.

In many ways, this is true; in other ways, it's an excuse to sit at home in lotus position, and do nothing at all.

Jorge takes a different tack and brings a breath of fresh air - indeed, he brings a thunderclap and a lightning bolt to shake us out of the old grooves we have gotten stuck in, lift us up and quite literally, inspire us to think afresh, to make new decisions, to pick up our power and TAKE ACTION.

Jorge says quite simply that he always wanted to be "a better person."

This never means that you're not good enough right now, or that there's anything whatsoever wrong with you, or me - or him.

What it means is that WE CAN DO BETTER.

So, so much better!

We can do more, we can experience more, we can create more, we can have MORE - of everything!

Personal development is the greatest game in the world, the best hobby to have and definitely the most fun you can have with your clothes on.

Jorge lights a fire under the rocket that is personal development and makes it what it always should have been - dynamic, forward pointing, POWERFUL.

Do you want to be "a better person" too?

For sure, I do!

Let's find out what we can really achieve, feel, experience and make happen when we ...

Grow Confident!

Silvia Hartmann

September 2015

Introduction

As I was growing up I always did wonder what it would be like being an adult. I used to think adults had all the fun in the world and being a child was "hard!" (Wrong!)

When I turned 18 and I had to face the fact that I was an "adult," I suddenly changed my mind about it. I learned that being a child, a teenager and an adult was a bit of the same, a challenge!!!

Why on this planet did some people make it seem so easy?

Did people change as times changed?

Then, it dawned on me that we all put this "mask" (or "masks") on and go through life "pretending" and "playing" at life - the game of life, let's call it.

To be quite frank and totally honest with you, I was in two minds and beyond confused at this point. I was terrified to ask questions, just in case I offended someone, so I remained quiet and put those questions on the back burner.

I carried on "living," "doing" and "following" the rest of the people, fitting in and forgetting about those questions I once wanted to ask.

Although I continued to observe and notice what was going on around me, I still remained mindful of others and did not ask the questions I wanted the answers to…

These questions were:

Are you happy?

Do you feel fulfilled?

Have your dreams come true?

What pearls of wisdom could you share with me so I too can be happy and fulfilled?

Have you found love?

Are you confident???

These 6 questions were there at all times. I just lacked the courage to ask them - in my teens and early 20's anyway.

When I finally found the courage to ask those questions, I was astounded to find that the answer to almost all these questions was negative.

People were in general lost and purposeless, but why? (Most of them anyway!)

I continued my quest, asking even more questions that led me to answers, which in turn got me asking even more questions, fulfilling the prophecy of the never ending cycle.

Why, why, oh why?

Why were people so lost and lacking in purpose in life when there is only one (that we are aware of!) and it is far too precious to waste and do nothing with it?

Was I following in my forefathers' footsteps and heading towards a life of "misery and sadness" and lack and loneliness and unhappiness?

What had to happen so I could put a stop to the curse that was becoming an epidemic in the people around me?

I cannot pinpoint the exact moment when it happened, but one day I was able to see it with clarity.

I was walking in my town's high street and noticed (with my professional and therapist's eyes) that everyone walked and acted as if they had nothing to strive for, nothing worth fighting or living for, as if they had no self-esteem or no confidence.

It was then that I had a flashback. I realised that I had broken away from that "vicious cycle" and I was now walking freely, the shackles had been taken off and I had forgotten about my quest of finding out what moved people or, in this case, what held them back.

That moment when I had those two images in front of me, what I was witnessing and what I had broken away from, I remembered a research project I had done for my studies a few years earlier, where I learned that people didn't perform well at work because of their "lack" of self-esteem and/or confidence.

So, that random day I made the decision to enlighten the world and share with them what I did to break away from that life of uncertainty, despair and no confidence.

There was only one thing left to do - remember what I did to move toward the life I always wanted, what allowed me to "wake up" and reach toward my goals.

That is how Growing Confident was born - when I noticed no-one ever told us how to "be" confident or more confident (if you had some confidence to begin with), with integrity and achieve our goals without affecting other people along the way.

I looked around and realised that self-help books always tell you that you can have your cake and eat it too. But not a single one of them ever says how you get the cake in the first place, which is what I am doing here… I am sharing with you how to get that cake!

They all tell you that you can have this or that or the other, and not one says how you move toward the right frame of mind so you can go looking for your cake and eat it once you have found it. (By the way, I am using the term 'cake' very metaphorically.)

I realised that there was a huge lack of information on how to really become/be or, as I like to call it, Grow Confident.

This lack of information then discourages people and sends them further into the abyss they are fighting to come out of in the first place.

My promise to you is that in each and every page of Growing Confident you will find a nugget of information that will help you move in the right direction and break away from the life you don't want, taking a step closer to the life you do want.

One word of advice though - whatever you do always starts with a decision. So what is your decision, what do you want from reading this book?

Over to you, your time is now.

The time for a decision to Grow Confident has come - make yours.

Jorge

How to use this book

Note: I encourage you to write a note (at the front or back of the book) to yourself and date it the very first day you start reading this book. Say something meaningful and important to yourself. This will help you track your evolution and journey into Growing Confident.

There is no right or wrong way to go about reading this book. If it helps, read it sequentially, pick one step at random or start with the one that excites you most, whichever way you feel most happy.

You can read it cover to cover, back to front, from the middle to the end, as long as you read it with an open mind and, most importantly, with an open heart.

In each chapter you will find:

1. A step for Growing Confident,
2. A quote relevant to the subject,
3. The content of the step,
4. My story - how I did that step,
5. Things to avoid with each step,
6. The exercises, and
7. A poem.

For the exercises I strongly encourage you to take your time to do each one of them. In fact, I encourage you to refrain from starting the next step if you have not completed the exercises from the previous step.

To do this I highly recommend that you tell someone you are reading a book on confidence, and that you invite them to make you accountable for your actions. Share with them what the exercises are, stressing that in order to move on to the next step and continue Growing Confident, you must finish each one of the exercises.

Is that a deal?

In my personal experience, I never had an accountability buddy or someone who could make me accountable for my actions or, in this case, completing the tasks or exercises in a book. So that was my downfall in the past, not now!

It is my commitment to you that you get the most value from this book, so take my advice and get an accountability buddy - ideally Grow Confident together.

Do each exercise to the letter. Read it twice or more to make sure you are doing it correctly.

Remember, confidence is not a race, it is a continuum of growth and process of evolution. You cannot take shortcuts or cheat your way to it. You will know when you are there, because everything seems effortless. In fact, everything is effortless.

Do the exercises more than once if it helps you discover more about yourself.

At the end of the book I invite you to read the note you made on the very first day you started reading the book. Notice the difference.

Prologue: Growing Confident

As clichéd as it may sound, life does begin outside your comfort zone.

You may have read it umpteen times if you are as big a fan of self-help books and personal development as I am.

They call it comfort zone, because it is cosy, warm, familiar and comfortable, but sadly no learning and growth take place in that "zone" or sphere where many of us hardly ever venture out of.

Growing Confident was the single best thing I have ever done. It has allowed me to be the person I always dreamed of, to be a role model and, most importantly, has allowed me to want to speak up and share with the world how to Grow Confident too.

When I was growing up I had dreams too. To those around me I was just a dreamer. I was doomed to be like everybody else around me and, quite frankly, they thought of me and saw me as another casualty of the system.

I will not lie, I too thought of myself like that.

As a teenager, after having experienced first-hand difficulties and challenges that almost got the best of me, I went from believing that only "adults" had all the fun to children and adults had all the fun and the world was against teenagers.

Now that I look back, it was then when I had my best learning times and those experiences shaped my future without me realising it. If I only knew how much those lessons would help me!

I went from being cynical about the grass being greener on the other side to acknowledging that the grass IS greener on the other side, so as long as you get off your butt and do what it takes to get over the fence and not only walk on the green grass but smell the flowers in the meadows and run freely in the fields of life.

Having Grown Confident has given me so much, so much more than I ever thought I could have.

It wasn't until I was writing the pages you are now reading that I realised how far I have come and this urge of gratitude came over me and I felt humbled by it.

As I already said in the introduction, it all starts with a decision, a decision that stems from so deep inside of you that pinpointing it would almost seem impossible. One thing I can say is that what will free you and move you towards freedom of the mind, heart and soul is already in you - you just don't know it yet.

So, I made my decision long ago, when many would have given up. Something so deep in me, so rooted and in my very core told me: "Do not give up just yet, the best is yet to come."

These words of hope I now share with you in these pages:

"DO NOT GIVE UP JUST YET, THE BEST IS YET TO COME."

After I made my decision and started my Growing Confident journey, within 9 months I had found love and, to make it even more "surreal," within 24 months I had moved not only countries but continents too.

Just because I decided to change something - what I did not know, I just knew something had to change.

Growing Confident isn't a quick fix to anyone's problems. If you have picked this book thinking this will be the case, I am sorry it isn't.

Growing Confident is about your growth as an individual, your evolution as a person and how you can transfer these life skills onto others. It is simple, it just starts with a decision, a choice, which is always up to you.

One thing I can assure you is that when you Grow Confident, nothing will seem impossible. On the contrary you almost become superhuman. You will not take NO for an answer, because you know your worth and you are the one who calls the shots.

Isn't this what being an adult, in fact human, is all about, being free, confident and in control of our lives?

If what you have read so far appeals to you, I welcome you to submerge yourself in the pages ahead. And at the same time I urge you to read with patience and put into practice what you read.

Growing Confident isn't about quick changes. It is about journeying into a new life, into a new you, and by overcoming your obstacles, limiting beliefs and fears, stepping into the new, better and more confident you.

So without further ado, your time is now, time to start Growing Confident.

Jorge

Basingstoke 20th August 2015

Step 1: Choose To Be Better

"One's philosophy is not best expressed in words; it is expressed in the choices one makes... and the choices we make are ultimately our responsibility."

Eleanor Roosevelt

Every story starts with a decision, a choice having to be made. Sometimes it is a conscious decision, other times it is an unconscious one.

Whether you are aware of it or not, when that decision is made, it is for the better.

Many people are unaware of their unconscious decisions. They even think of destiny guiding them, their guardian angel or a guiding star.

However, there comes a point in our lives, more often than not it is after the age of 18, when we are "adults", or in some cases when misfortune strikes, that we own our decisions.

We consciously start taking decisions and choosing what we will and will not do. We start thinking of our "ideal" career path, "perfect" partner, "dream" home, etc., etc., etc.

So, this being said, do we ever consciously or unconsciously choose to be better? To be more and add more value to people's lives?

You do not need to answer this question just yet. I will, however, suggest you do it either now or later.

Explore your life up to now. Have you decided to be a better person and do what is best and right for every human being in your life? On the planet? If you have, then congratulations. Keep reading and continue your great work.

By now, you must be asking yourself: "What has choosing to be better got to do with confidence?" The answer is very simple, EVERYTHING.

When you are congruent with your choices to be a better individual and adding value to people's lives, you operate from a completely different realm. You work from a realm of integrity, helpfulness and love.

We all have heard the saying: "We are better together!" It is so very true though.

Let me ask you a question. Has there ever been a time in your life when you would have given your life for someone's sake? To help them and nurture them and prevent them from harm?

If you answered yes, I honour you! Because this is true altruism: to wish you could take someone's hurt and pain and misfortune away, to make it yours so they don't suffer any longer.

This is what I refer to as choosing to be better.

The title “Choose to be better” may put some people off. It is OK, they perhaps don’t understand the concept of solidarity and altruism, or may even think they know it all. In reality, like everything in life, we find ourselves making assumptions that we know it all, when we haven’t even started to scratch the surface.

I too, once thought I knew it all. More of that later…

A few years back, when I immersed myself fully in the self-development world, I came across a motivational public figure. At this time he had been dead for a few years, but his philosophy and wisdom have outlived him. His name is Jim Rohn and in one of his many seminars he once said: “Do not wish it was easier, wish you were better!”

I have to be totally frank here, I didn’t get it at first. I kept blaming my tools and everybody else.

Now I can see clearly what he meant. There isn’t anything wrong with the tools or people for that matter. I just didn’t know how to use those tools. I didn’t have the knowledge to put into practice what I wanted to do. I was too arrogant to admit I was wrong and it was a lot easier to pass the blame onto somebody else.

Can you relate to this?

Have you ever wished life was easier? That your job was easier?

I bet you didn’t get very far. If you did, well done. Because with that mentality I didn’t get very far. Now that I look back, I am able to see how much it has hindered me and held me back. But it is OK, I had to go through that experience to learn what I now know and avoid making the same mistakes. And if I find myself making those mistakes again, then I haven’t fully learned what being better means.

If you have got this far reading, instead of wishing things were easier, now say out loud: “I wish I was better”… Say it many times over and over and over again.

I WISH I WAS BETTER.

I WISH I WAS BETTER.

I WISH I WAS BETTER.

At this point, I want to clarify by stating this: you are not (nor me for that matter) saying that there is something wrong with you. On the contrary, you are saying you can be a whole lot better, be more and most importantly add immense value to everyone in your life.

Isn’t that a great place to be? Adding value to people’s lives day in and day out, constantly.

So far, we have talked about choosing to be better, and now we can marry it with being and Growing Confident.

When you know you are doing your absolute 100%, because you have made the decision to be better than you were yesterday and add value to people’s lives, there is nothing in this world that can bring you down.

If something goes wrong when you operate from this philosophy, no-one can bring you down. People's words and actions will slide down and mean nothing, simply because you know in yourself (which is always the best feedback you can get) you did all you could. You did your enjoyable best.

Once you get into the rhythm of improving yourself, by wishing you were better each and every day, you will not only Grow Confident but you will also be getting great results in every area of your life.

Friendships will be stronger, romance will be better, colleagues will like you more, and employers will give you more responsibilities and maybe even a promotion. If you are a business owner, your employees will do anything for you because you are their role model. You inspire them and motivate them.

Wishing you were better doesn't mean you wish you were someone you aren't, or someone else, but a better and improved version of who you are.

Here is another quote by Jim Rohn, and this is what really made me wish I was better. Why? Because it simply scared me… It was just too true. He once said: "You are the average of the 5 people closest to you." And if that wasn't scary enough, he also said: "Your salary is the average of the 5 people closest to you."

This brought wishing or choosing to be better a lot closer to home. At this point I decided to be honest with myself and I took a good look at the people around me. I decided to sit silently and listen to what they were saying, how they were saying it, and what they said about money…

What I heard was not what I wanted to hear. I must be 100% honest, it was just the reality. Did I continue on the same road as everybody else, that was leading me to the same destination, which didn't quite appeal to me? Or did I choose to change and be better?

I hope at this moment you realise what decision I made. I chose to be better, not because that egotistic side of me felt I was better, but because I wanted to make a difference. I just didn't have the tools I needed to make that a reality.

Making this decision not only was one of the best decisions I have ever made, but it gave me tons and tons of confidence. I was able to say NO to invites that would have led me away from my dream, which is to help you.

I would not have had the courage to say "No, thank you." One simple decision gave me the energy to see it all through.

The confidence was a by-product of that. It wasn't expected, it just landed by my side and served me greatly to be able to share it with you.

Here is a list of how you can choose to be better:

- Being a better friend,
- Being a better lover,
- Being a better child,
- Being a better parent,
- Being a better employee,
- Being a better employer,
- Being a better neighbour,
- Being a better listener,
- Being a better sibling,
- Being a better civilian,
- Being a better person.

These are just ideas of how you can be better, and forget the idea of comparing or contrasting. When you make a decision from and based in pure love only, you will not need to be praised or told how you have become better, simply because it will be a part of you that you just see as normal.

Choosing to be better needn't be ego-based or to prove a point.

Choose To Be Better: My Story

If you haven't heard of me before this book, then now is a good time to tell you a bit about me and my story.

I was born in 1983, in Panama City. I was the child of a single mother, who gave birth to me at the age of 19. She came from the provinces, so had very little education and her main aim in life was to survive each day as it came.

I have very little recollection of the first few years of my life. I grew up thinking and believing my aunt was my mother, saw her children as my cousins, which makes no sense at all.

Suddenly towards the end of the 80's this father figure came into my life. It was all a blur. He was introduced as my father and I totally believed it.

Then came the invasion by the Americans to arrest Colonel Noriega. This was 1989. I had gone from being in a modest 1 bedroom home to a larger 1 room house, where things were arranged nicely to give the appearance of having several rooms.

In 1991, out of nowhere, came my little brother. Needless to say, I stopped being the little baby and became the older brother of the son of my mother's love of her life.

I grew up accepting poverty. I was told that some people were born in money and others weren't, and that I was one of those.

I was a good and obedient son, otherwise there would be consequences. And boy, did I fear those consequences.

As a child I used to love and look forward to Christmas. For one day I forgot I was poor and poverty altogether. Christmas was not only a time for celebration (in the heat of the tropics!), but it was a time to dream and be abundant. It didn't matter if it was only one day.

I remember my mother would get up bright and early on Christmas Eve and drag me along to the shops, to buy me new clothes which were expected to last a whole year!!! We would then go and buy the groceries and presents, and... I would be taken to my very favourite burger bar, because it was time to celebrate and they had been saving all year to be able to splash out and spend it all in just one day.

My mother would spend the rest of the night baking cakes, making salads and cooking the turkey (which is the best I have had to date!). I would be the typical child, all over the place, not allowing her to get on with her tasks and chores.

I would fantasise about my presents. Would I get the presents I wanted? What would my neighbours get?

Now that I look back, my parents sacrificed a lot so that that day could be the best each and every year.

After my brother's birth things did change, as they do. We went from 3 mouths to feed to 4, all of that in under a year. And let's not forget to mention my brother was born in November, so his first Christmas wasn't as abundant as mine, because the priorities had changed.

What has this got to do with choosing to be better?

Absolutely everything…

As I went through my school years and into my early teens, I became a bit of a hermit. I started to notice we were not only poor, but poorer than most in our neighbourhood.

Strangely enough I didn't have many friends. At school they were only peers and nothing else. At home I didn't want to play with the other children. We were different, we wanted different things and, just before I forget, I liked boys too!

This didn't make matters any easier, if anything it made them a whole lot harder for me. Being called names didn't appeal to me, I wasn't the strongest or fittest. I had no interests, I had no dreams - in essence I was dead in a living body.

I just didn't know it.

I lived for the day, and as the day died out I had nothing to look forward to for the next day, or the next, or the next - never mind the year ahead or 10 years hence.

Years passed, as they do, at first slowly, and then suddenly you are in secondary school.

Many things had changed by now. I was meeting new people, learning a lot and still felt ashamed of my background. All my new mates at secondary school were much better off than me, so I created two personalities. The one that pretended at school, and the real me.

I had friends for a whole 6 hours, Monday to Friday, but had no-one at home. My parents were just that, parents. I never felt I could tell them anything without there being consequences.

Every action would most definitely get a reaction. So I was silent at home. There were two things I could do and I think I did them well. I got rewarded for one!

Those two things were: watching television - watching TV programmes where absolutely everyone was perfect in every single way, rich and intelligent. Life always gave them a good hand in the game of life.

The other thing I did very well was reading. It was one of those things you had to do when you had no friends and the TV programme that was on was not your cup of tea.

Reading helped me get good marks (not the best, but good enough to be called "intelligent"). My parents' idea of a good reward was to get me a set of encyclopaedias, which cost them a fortune.

I wish I could say I was over the moon with it, but I wasn't. Something else would have sufficed.

So, my double life continued through secondary school. It got worse - all my mates wanting to go to my house (as you do!), and me saying my mother didn't like strangers in her house. But it was OK to go to theirs, enjoying a better life by proxy.

My reading and studying got better, I had to channel my energy somehow. In my neighbourhood my neighbours and I still had nothing in common. The fact that my little brother, who had grown quite a bit by then, once said: "I wish our next door neighbour was my brother and not you," didn't quite help the way I felt about many things.

In the long run those encyclopaedias saved me from madness. I learned so much, and started to dream.

I saw these encyclopaedias as a tele-transporting channel where I could escape my life and go to wild and incredible destinations and I could be anything I wanted to be. For once I dreamed of a better life.

You would think that by now, after reading with my new best friends, the encyclopaedias, I would be much happier and comfortable with myself, but I wasn't.

In 1999, many things happened, which I shall omit for the sake of space (this is a whole book itself). My whole life and belief system was shaken and it ended upside down.

I did what worked best by then. I had been doing it for 16 years, it was a proven strategy. I continued pretending and hiding and wishing I was no longer …

The year 2000 came, and with it the darkest hour of my soul. I lost the will to live, there was no point. I was dead as it was, why pretend any longer? Only one thing could save me, and that would be an early grave.

For some reason I found myself in front of a psychiatrist and a psychologist. They were going to help, so I thought! I started on antidepressants. I did not know I was depressed. I just needed to take something to make the pain and ache go away and make me "better" and "normal" for once, and for the first time in my life.

I continued taking these antidepressants for a few weeks. No-one but my mother knew what I was going through, a mother who prior to that had said: "I had you on a pedestal, and now you are nothing to me!"

Yep, it was said, it was heard and remembered at that point. The tablets didn't seem to be working - I felt worse. In my last year at school, just before university, nothing seemed to be going right for me. I had no-one, I was dead and I did not know what to do.

I cry as I type this, because I made it through and I am here for whomever feels like I once felt.

I was very lonely, I had no voice, and at 2 o'clock on the 27th of March 2000, I took all of my antidepressants out of their packaging and spread them on the table, counted them, the two types I was taking. There were 47 and I put them all in my hand, looked at them, grabbed a glass of water and, with a deep breath in, took them all, right in front of my brother.

I silently went to bed, hoping to never wake up.

Five hours later, my mother woke me up. I was out of it. I wasn't aware of the time, I just felt dizzy and airy.

I was left wondering what would have happened had my mother not woken me up. I will never know. One thing is for sure - I give my mother all the credit for having given me life, not once but twice.

So, I woke up on the 28th of March feeling grateful and lucky to have made it through. Many days passed before I told my mother what I had done.

In all of this confusion and dizziness I found the courage and strength to speak to someone, a complete stranger at the time, who then became a great mentor. I just opened my heart and let it all out. I had been carrying almost 17 years of baggage which I didn't need nor did I want, but it was there. Talking, it all came out and as the words came out of my mouth I felt lighter and lighter in myself.

It was this day, after all I went through, that I made the conscious decision to be better and more, not for me but for those who like me are trapped in a prison created by nothing and fed by our fears and losses in the battlefield of life.

It was this very day that I let go of my shame and baggage and I said yes to life and being alive and living and love and options and possibilities and dreams and me.

I chose to be better so I could tell my story and share with you and the world what is possible.

Choose To Be Better: Things To Avoid

There isn't a right or wrong way to choose to be better. However, I would strongly suggest, when you make this decision, avoid the following:

1. Do not do it to prove a point to anyone,
2. Do not do it to show how much better you are,
3. Do not do it for financial gains,
4. Do not do it to impress someone,
5. Do not do it to get revenge over someone,
6. Do not do it for the praise,
7. Do not do it for vanity,
8. Do not do it to hurt other people.

I have noticed that when you choose to be better, everything else is but the by-product of it. Do it because you want the best for every person you meet, do it because you want the world to be a better place.

Choose To Be Better: The Exercises

1. Journaling

If you haven't already got a journal, I strongly encourage you to get a journal and start writing your ideas, wants and desires in life.

Goal setting is very important when you choose to make a difference in the world. You need to know what steps you will follow, otherwise it is pointless.

When you set a deadline for a goal, your unconscious mind gets to work and finds ideas and possibilities to make it happen.

I am sure you have heard the saying: "A goal is a dream with a deadline."

When you write your goals and ideas on a regular basis, you are able to monitor what really matters to you. You notice patterns, and you are able to see solutions.

You become a dreamer, and when you dream you activate new neurological pathways. And let's not forget to mention that your mind doesn't recognise what is real and what isn't!

Use a journal, and allow it to be your new best friend.

You can even write questions. Leave it alone for a few minutes, hours or days and then allow your unconscious mind to give you the answers you seek.

The ways in which you can use a journal are endless.

Do it, you will see the benefits.

Any notepad will do. Keep it private and with you at all times.

2. Read Biographies

As you will remember, I loved, and still to this date I love, reading a good book. There are endless and countless biographies and autobiographies out there.

We live in an era where there is so much information available to us. The only thing we must do is to look for it.

When you were growing up, who inspired you? Who was your real life hero?

Did your parents ever tell you the story of a person they ever met or knew about who made a difference in people's lives?

Who would you like to know more about?

If you don't know of any historical person that could be a role model to you, ask people who inspired them and why?

Read, read, and read. I could not stress it and highlight it enough. Again, reading activates new neurological pathways and makes you more knowledgeable and interesting as a person.

You win from every angle.

I could give you a list of numerous people, but it isn't my place. You have to find them for yourself and discover the connection between you and that person.

That's when the magic happens.

Do it, do it now.

3. Read and watch the news

I will hold my hands in the air and say it: "I do not read and watch the news enough."

However, when I do, I discover new ways in which I can be better for those around me.

When you are aware of what is going on around you, it awakens that curiosity (of which we will talk more later) in you and you start thinking of ways to contribute, give back and make a positive impact in people's lives.

We are very fortunate that we can access the news at the touch of a screen. Never have we ever been so close to the news. We can access it live, as it happens.

This gives us that opportunity to be more current on how we can be of service, being better, choosing to be better rather. Start now.

I ask myself this question constantly.

What can I do right now so I can make a difference in someone's life? Or,

What can I do right now so I can make someone's day? Or,

What can I do right now so I can make someone happy?

You see, when you are current and aware of what is happening in the world, your choices can have a very positive impact in someone's life.

You never know, one day it may even be you. Why not make a deposit in the bank of kindness (or niceness, as I like to call it!).

4. Remember Your Better Moments

Think of a time you chose to be better and made someone's day

When we remember nice memories or happy thoughts, we are able to live that experience all over again.

I encourage you to remember a time, either recent or some time ago, and go through that experience in your head.

What day of the week was it? Where were you? What were you doing? Who was with you? What was going through your mind?

And then what happened?

How did you make that person's day?

How did you feel afterwards?

As you bring back that memory I would like you to stay there for a few minutes. Replay it multiple times as you can or wish.

What was that person's reaction?

Did they expect you to help them or do something for them?

Continue to absorb that memory and even write it down in your new journal.

Now that you have gone through that experience in your head, I invite you to visit many more.

Or even better, why not go out there and create new positive experiences like that one?

You see, when you act from a place of kindness and love, that gives you super strength and confidence to do and make anything possible.

Do it more often and you will make it part of your daily routine, to the point it will become a habit and part of your behaviour.

5. Give To Charity

I understand not everyone is capable of donating to charity or volunteering some of their time. However, charity goes beyond that. It is an act of kindness, making the unexpected possible in someone's life, smiling at the lonely and sad, giving a flower to an older lady as she passes by.

To me charity is about sharing hope and kindness with others and expecting nothing back.

If, on the other hand, you are able to donate money to a good cause, by all means go ahead. 50 cents or 20 pence can make a huge difference in someone's life. Or if you are able to give some of your time for free and volunteer for a local charity, I urge you to do it.

To see the real gratitude in someone's face is worth much more than all the money in the world.

Charity is much more than giving your spare change. It is about care and solidarity with a cause much greater than you and me.

I Choose To Be Better

Yesterday served me not!
I had challenges,
So now, what do I do?
Do I hold on to what didn't work?
Or do I move forward?
My head isn't in the right place,
Timing is everything in this game they call life.
Options, decisions, choices and alternatives.
Do I hold onto what didn't work?
Or do I move forward?
I am at a crossroad,
Years of pain and hurt,
I couldn't bear any more,
So now, what do I do?
I wish life was as easy as they make it to be.
No-one told me when I signed my contract,
I would be served this hand.
Oh, what should I endeavour now?
I tried and I failed,
I lived and I loved,
I gave it all and lost it all.
So now, I let go of that invisible chain,
I look at life in the eyes, and
Say: I choose to be better,
Before, I thought I was weak,
Though now, I have found my strength,
I choose to be better,
Not because I have to, but because I want to,
Selfishness and ego betrayed,
Life taught me a lesson.
I choose to be better,
Not because I was forced,
But because I now know,
I count, my life matters,

And what better way to honour life
Than to share it and honour it.
I choose to be better
To make a difference in the world,
To bring forth the light
And love and joy
I choose to be better
Because now I know I am in control,
I choose what I do and where I go,
I choose to be free,
I choose to be me.

Step 2: Curiosity

"We keep moving forward, opening new doors, and doing new things, because we're curious and curiosity keeps leading us down new paths."

Walt Disney

In this step I want to share with you my favourite subject in the entire universe. Curiosity, being curious and what it does for you.

Although I have mentioned I didn't have many friends as I was growing up, there was one thing that kept me somewhat sane; that my friend was using my imagination, which stemmed from being curious.

Curiosity, to me, is like a bridge which connects the impossible with the possible, dreams with reality, fiction with facts. Curiosity is what allows the artist to create masterpieces, the philosopher to take concepts and ideas and make them fresher and current.

When you are curious you become interested in people, so curiosity adds to what we have talked about previously. You choose to be better because you are curious about things.

What would my life look like if I serve other people?

What would my children's life look like if I am making a difference in people's lives?

These and many other questions do come from curiosity.

I remember a few instances as a child when I didn't understand what was being said and because I wanted to know and find out what the adults were talking about, I would ask out of curiosity.

Many of the greatest inventions we possess in today's society came to be because one person was curious about light, a talking machine, an object to see pictures, an object in which we could fly and go to outer space.

Just consider for a moment if those thinkers of the past hadn't being curious. What would our lives look like right now?

I can answer it for you…

We would have no electricity, no potable water, no landlines, no mobile phones, no computers, no airplanes, no boats, no trains, no cars, no internet. We would have virtually nothing of what we now have and life as we know it would be totally different.

What did they all have in common? They were courageous, they believed, they dreamed, they were focused, but most importantly they had every ounce of confidence in themselves. And they wanted to add value to people's lives, so they did.

Am I painting the picture for you? Do you hear what I am saying? How does it sit with you?

Being curious is a gift. Your curiosity is totally different to mine. What you find interesting may not be so for me and vice versa.

When you are curious, many doors open. You are able to use your imagination, ask questions that not many would ask. And when you ask questions, you get answers. These answers then trigger more questions, which lead to more answers, to new knowledge, and you become more inquisitive, more interested, more interesting. Your brain again starts creating new neurological pathways, and you win 100% from every angle.

Do you remember when you were a child?

How inquisitive you were about everything? You would ask questions non-stop to people you knew and those you didn't know.

At this point I would like to make a comment, which is directed to those of you who are parents or are planning to have children.

In my many years of observation, call it curiosity if you may, I have noticed that children are not as curious and inquisitive as we once were.

This is the result of the technological advancement we have experienced in the last two or so decades. Also, parents are prohibiting their children to be curious, punishing them if they explore or try something new.

What do you think this does to their confidence?

Will they grow up to be confident and adventurous?

I do not think so.

If you are a parent, please, I beg of you, teach, show your child how to be curious, be curious with them. They will thank you later for it.

Another example of how our curiosity is undermined by others is how we are told it is wrong to talk to strangers. This belief clings on to us for a lifetime, to the point that we cannot communicate properly. We are unable to ask questions, we dislike public speaking, we don't like social events, and the list goes on and on and on.

Let me clarify, I do understand especially parents' concerns around their children talking to strangers and the dangers it may have. But when you explain in detail that some people may have bad intentions, not all, and that it is OK to talk to "strangers" as long as you are safe when you do so, it would make life a lot easier when they grow up.

More often than not our curiosity is sent to sleep because those before didn't understand it. They were told make-believe stories about being curious.

There is nothing wrong with being curious. It propels you to dreaming, to wanting more in life, to add value to the life of others. And by doing so you become more confident.

Everyone wins.

When everyone is a winner, there are no losers, and as a result people are happier. When people are happier, they become more effective. When people are more effective, they become more productive. When people are more productive, economies boom. When economies boom, there are enough resources for everyone. When we have more resources for everyone, we can eradicate so many negative things from the planet.

All of this is possible because we are curious. So far in 2015 there are around 7 billion human beings of all ages. I believe the largest demographic group is the baby boomers who were born post 1946.

Just imagine for a second if each one of us was to be curious once a day, twice a week or three times per month. Over the period of a year, if we take the last example, that would be 36 acts of curiosity per person each year. That would be 252 billion acts of curiosity annually. What could that do for the world?

It would make it a lot better and easier for everyone to live. New ideas and concepts would be born, technology would be even better than we know it, research would be much more advanced than it is, and cures to countless illnesses and diseases would be found.

What would this do for us?

A lot - we would be strong, optimistic and guess what? Confident too.

As I write this I just remembered the saying: "Curiosity killed the cat." Really? It didn't kill it. What killed it was the lack of it. He was bored!!! The poor cat had nothing to look forward to, he was striving for nothing.

We all have something unique and precious to share with the world (more of that later), though we can only discover what it is, when we are curious about it. What is it that I can give to this world so I can add value to it and its people?

How powerful is this?

How will you feel when you find out that your work is making a difference in someone's life?

Exactly - confident, strong, happy.

After reading these lines, what will you do differently? How will you go about being curious? Will you be curious with your children (if you are a parent)?

I encourage you to read this step several times, and be very curious about it. What can you discover in here that will spark your curiosity once more?

Being curious isn't being nosey, as we have been told many times. It will not kill you, your cat or anyone's cat for that matter.

On the contrary, being curious will allow you to be more explorative, interested in how things work, why things don't work. You will come up with new ideas, you will find ways to add value to everyone's lives and as you do so, you live an abundant life. This abundance gives you strength and confidence and brings happiness that we all so desperately need.

When you become curious you are open to a host of possibilities, options and answers. You become a child again and you are able to enjoy life once more, through the eyes of innocence and purity.

Curiosity: My Story

Although I was curious most of my childhood, I would say I became really curious about life in general in my late teens.

When I started university at the age of 17, it was a completely clean slate. I had already made the decision to be better and make a difference in people's lives.

So, I found myself talking to people, finding out more about them, being there for them, being curious and interested about them, while remaining respectful.

This phase of my life truly was a new beginning for me. I had a wound that was slowly but surely healing. I was doing my best to add value to people's lives while getting over my not so distant memory.

I can honestly say that being curious was one of the best things that I did in those days. I made the best friends anyone could wish for. We created a strong bond and almost felt like family.

Being curious allowed me to learn more about various subjects at university, encouraged me to find out more about me, who I was.

It was this self-discovery journey that gave me strength to question things, authorities, concepts and ideas, and find my own voice.

When I realised I had a voice, I felt empowered, I felt complete and for the first time in my life I was able to see myself as a role model. I had no idea who would want me to be their role model, but I knew I could inspire people because I was not a prisoner anymore. By prisoner, I mean prisoner of the self; that cell we created years and years back, and with time we just make bolder and stronger and almost unbreakable.

As I said, I did not know whose role model I could have been in those days. The answer came some years later.

It is worth mentioning that I did not complete my university studies. I found myself getting on a plane, almost 3 years after I thought there was no point. My curiosity landed me in the right place, at the right time, with the right person.

I simply met the most incredible person, who saw me for me and wanted me for me. He offered me two things I will never forget. He offered me love and the opportunity to join him in Europe - there were no catches, no small print.

Life, fate and destiny for once were plotting in my favour. I had a rebirth, I had friends, I was curious and I was learning much more than I ever thought I could.

Oh, how blessed I felt.

My life finally was going in the right direction, simply because I had done two things, which I have shared with you so far:

- I chose to be better. I said goodbye to stupid, old and useless paradigms. I knew I was worth something. I didn't know what it was, but I knew it was much more that I had known before. And,

- I was curious - about life, people, myself, the world, everything - absolutely everything. I wanted to know more about love. I was curious about it and it landed me in one of the most romantic love stories I have ever known, even if I may say so. I had to learn to be even more curious when I started learning a new language. Yes, English is not my first language. Being curious allowed me to master it.
- Just imagine what you will learn when I share with you the other 8 steps. My goodness, you will be a confidence projector.

Going back to being someone's role model. 5 or so years later I was having a cyber-conversation with one of my former university peers, and Dessy, her name, said to me: "I always used to look up to you. You exuded this air of confidence about you. You learned effortlessly and everyone liked you."

When I read those lines, I did not know what positive effect I had had in people's lives. I was harsh and cruel to myself (like many of us are!) and I quite honestly thought that I was just a normal bloke, leading a normal life, doing normal stuff - being normal, in a nutshell. Not once did I ever see myself as a role model until then.

I was doing what was normal to me. I did not, consciously at least, think that I would be someone's role model or that people would look up to and want to be like me!

Now, with the knowledge and experience I have and the mistakes I have made, I can see how important my actions are, not so much because of what people may say, but how it impacts in their lives.

Naivety is one of those words that comes to mind. I used to think that the only role models we had were our parents and teachers and people in history books, because they had had years and decades of experience and they knew what they were doing and talking about.

I was wrong, very wrong. We can all make a difference in someone's life.

I learned to embrace each day as if it were my last. I look at people with such interest and curiosity. I look at animals in nature, plants in the wild. I am curious about what happens in my body, what my thoughts are like (we all know the impact those thoughts can have in our day, week, month and year).

I am curious about learning something new each and every day.

Here is a very brief list of what I am curious about on a regular basis:

- I am curious what the weather is going to be like,
- I am curious about what to eat for breakfast, lunch and dinner,
- I am curious to know if my body will be able to process the food I want to eat,
- I am curious as to whether I need to exercise more,
- I am curious about what my pet is thinking,
- I am curious about my thoughts (this very second!),
- I am curious about how I can make more of a difference,
- I am curious about helping others,
- I am curious about curiosity,
- I am curious about love,
- I am curious about life,
- I am curious about my family's well being,
- I am curious about my friend's happiness,
- I am curious as to what tomorrow will bring,
- I am curious about 10, 15, 20 years hence,
- I am curious about the past,
- I am curious about learning skills that I can use to be of even more service,
- I am curious about my health,
- I am curious about everything.

This curiosity allows me to pick up the phone and ask my friends and family how they are, and help them if they need me.

This curiosity allows me do a reality check, and honestly ask myself: "Do I have all the skills necessary to have a positive impact in the lives of millions? If not, what can I do?" I become curious about finding new ways and avenues to close that gap and get those extra resources so I can help even more people.

This curiosity gives me the strength to get up and out of bed first thing in the morning, so I too can work on myself, my fitness, education, development, evolution and create the life I know I deserve. And you too deserve a great live.

This curiosity makes me curious about love. What can I do to love even more people? How can my love touch someone's life and inspire them to work towards their dreams and wants in life?

This curiosity has given me the courage to put fingers to keyboard and give you what you need, so you too can Grow Confident and attain the excellence you deserve.

This curiosity has given me the energy to say no. When things have tried to derail me from my path, it has kept me focused and on track.

Curiosity has played a great part in my life, and I urge you to become curious, right now! Just do it… Ask yourself, what can I be curious about?

Be curious about curiosity itself?

What is curiosity?

I actually do not even know the true meaning of curiosity… I will get it right away.

According to The Oxford English Dictionary, curiosity is: "A strong desire to know or learn something."

A curious person, however, is eager to know or learn something.

What comes with curiosity only you can measure. I can give you a million reasons why you should be curious, but it isn't until you yourself embrace that curiosity, that you can start reaping the rewards.

Many people throughout my life have commented on my "intelligence." I am not intelligent at all. My grades and marks were very average (OK, let's admit a bit above average), but I was not one of the most remarkable students. What I was and still am is curious about things, how they work and how I can use them in my daily life.

If I do not understand something, I look it up or ask someone who can help with it. Curiosity is what allows me and propels me to do just that.

And yes, when you are curious about things, you gain knowledge, which you can use to inspire others, to earn a good living, but most importantly to Grow Confident. So when you are asked a question, you can say with confidence: "This is it, and here is the evidence."

Curiosity: Things To Avoid

There isn't much to be avoided when you are curious. Just be mindful about other people and how they may interpret your intentions.

One word of advice: avoid being arrogant or pedantic at all costs, if you can. Again this is all down to people's interpretations.

Remember, curiosity did NOT kill the cat. Boredom did.

I am sitting here, writing on a laptop, created by man. That says how much potential you have. You are the best computer ever made - use it wisely.

Be curious about everything you can think of … Who knows, you may be the solution to many of our "problems."

Curiosity: The Exercises

When you are curious, the possibilities are almost endless. You can do anything, anywhere, anytime, with anyone.

I promise I will be gentle with this section as it is my favourite part of Growing Confident.

1. Be Curious Like A Child.

If you have children, nephews/nieces, godchildren, or if you are around children, watch them (please proceed with caution, around children, as things are a bit over the top these days, and I wouldn't like to receive any complaints about adults around children acting strangely!). See their faces, the excitement with which they want to know about things like the grass (Why is it green?), butterflies (Why do they fly?), cars (Why do they have 4 wheels, and not 2?).

Put yourself in that child's shoes. See what they see, hear what they hear, feel what they feel…

How do you feel in yourself now that you have experienced life and curiosity through the eyes of a child (again!)?

I highly encourage you to absorb and really take in any lessons from this exercise.

What do you feel? Freedom? More alive? Curious? Happier? Creative? Knowledgeable?

Do it as often as you can. Be a child more often and curiosity will be second nature.

Now that you have a journal, write down your ideas, your feelings. What are you curious about? Did you remember something you used to be curious about as a child?

Curiosity is a doorway to a world of endless possibilities. It allows you to dream, to want, to be, have and do.

2. Watch The News!

Yes! Here it is again. This time look at the news from a different angle. Rather than finding ways of making a difference, I invite you to discover ways to be curious about what is happening in that part of the world. Why is it happening?

If there is tragedy in a faraway country or village, be curious about ways in which people can help. How can you help?

What needs to happen so everyone is cared for?

Use this exercise to brainstorm ideas of curiosity and how to find solutions to riddles and problems.

Again, write it down on your journal. You never know what this may become. It could end up being a project to really make a difference in the world.

3. Take A Long Walk!

Ideally this exercise is to be done alone, in the woods, either first thing in the morning or in the evening, when things are quieter in nature. Avoid taking cameras, or mobile phones with you. You want to be distraction-free.

Walk and watch the plants and flowers. What stories are they telling you? What are the colours? What are the smells like? Have you been in this woodland before? Or is it your first time?

Is there a river or a brook nearby? What does it sound like? Or have you decided to go to the beach? Is it a sandy or pebble beach? What are the sounds of the waves crashing against the shore like? What stories is it telling you?

Are there any animals in the vicinity? Can you see them? What are they doing? What do they sound like? Are they looking after their offspring? Are they watching you in a curious manner? Wondering who you are?

Are there any other people nearby? If so, what are they doing? Are they talking to one another? Are they talking to you? Are you going to talk to them? Are they curious about their surroundings?

Are there any houses? Or buildings either near or in the distance? Can you hear any machinery or cars or planes? Are you feeling curious as to whether you are all alone in the woods?

I highly suggest you do this exercise on a weekly basis, in different locations. And once you feel comfortable and know what you are doing, take someone with you and show them how they too can be curious about nature and situations in general.

4. Learn A New Skill

Yes, you have read it well. Learn a new skill.

Has there ever been a skill or technique or anything you wanted to find out more about?

If so, go ahead and do it. This curiosity-based learning experience will show you how learning can be fun. When we are children we are petrified at the idea of being tested on our knowledge, and we learn to dislike learning.

On the other hand, when you learn because you want to, and no-one will be measuring your knowledge at the end of it, you learn to fall in love with learning again.

The more you learn and know, the better you become at what you do. And guess what, more neurological pathways are formed, come on! You do become a real winner, you win from every angle.

This may be the gateway to a new, better and more exciting job. It could be the stepping stone to that promotion you always wanted, more money, more authority. And you get to be a role model.

Once you learn a new skill in the pockets of time you have, you become better at personal management. You see options and possibilities where you saw none before.

You grow as a person, and more confident too.

5. Write A Story About Curiosity

If you are like me, at this point you are probably screaming: "I can't write a story, I can't spell, let alone write a story."

I urge you to take a deep breath.

Do this several times.

As you breathe in deeply, drift into a land of options and dreams. And fantasy is available everywhere, you can breathe it in, you can eat it, you can touch it. It is your muse and it is here to stay.

Don't think about it and grab a pen and paper. Do not rationalise what you start writing, go with the flow and do not stop until the story is complete. You will know when it is complete because this is your story. No-one else's.

A day or so later, read what you have written. What is the story telling you? Where is it taking place? Who is the hero? Is there a villain? What are you most curious about in the story?

What needs to happen to make the story more compelling? Use your curiosity to bring the story together.

Or, it may be the case that the story is perfect as it is.

If it isn't, I like to use the analogy of a cooking recipe. You follow the instructions to the letter and it comes to the crucial moment in the recipe - the seasoning. Let's use the example of salt. If you add too little it's too bland, you add too much it's too salty, so it can be a slow and gradual process. Each time you add salt to your dish you do not know what you will get, until you get the perfect seasoning.

Writing a story and being curious about it makes it a lot more interesting, for yourself, and the reader (if you are an author).

A variation to this exercise is to take a story. It could be well known or a lesser known one. Play with the characters and setting, be really curious about everything. Think what was going through the author's mind when he/she wrote the book. Is it a biographical story? Are the characters strong enough? Or could you make them stronger? And make the story much more exciting?

When you become really comfortable with this game (because let's be real, this is just a game to tap into the realms of curiosity), you may even discover you like writing more than you thought you did.

I highly recommend taking a journal with you at all times. You can have more than 1. I personally have various, in which I record different things - a dream journal, a behaviour journal, an ideas journal.

The whole idea is to capture your ideas, things you are curious about and want to know more about.

Do it at first weekly, then daily if you can. Be curious, make a difference and Grow Confident.

Curiosity Is Freedom

I wandered lonely as a cloud,
Said a poet once.
What a beautiful way
To go about your day.
Listening to the wind
Speaking to the world.
Curiosity - oh, what would I do without you in my life?
When I wake up I find you so deep in me,
I cannot stop wondering what life will be like for the day.
People, what a beautiful extension of who I am.
I see their faces and I want to know them,
I live for them and to make their day.
Animals, God's work and creation.
Communicate I wish I could,
Good day Mr Cat, good afternoon to you Mr Pigeon, I would say.
And plants? Oh you incredible greenery,
You give so much to me, you keep me alive,
Respect you and honour you I want,
Save the planet and your cousins around the globe.
What a dull vacuum life is without curiosity!
I would not be as happy as I am,
Curiosity is freedom,
A freedom that comes from God,
A freedom that comes from within.
Oh, what will my day be like?
I can't stop but wonder what surprises are coming my way.
I am curious, it is my right.
A life without curiosity isn't a life worth living for,
I am curious, therefore I am free.
Oh what a joy, for I can be,
Oh what a joy, for I am
I am curious, therefore I am.

Step 3: Healing the Past

> ***"Healing is a matter of time, but it is sometimes also a matter of opportunity."***
>
> ***Hippocrates***

This section will help you understand the power of letting go of the past, how evolving what happened and not holding on to it could be the solution to all your "problems."

Letting go of the past is what has given me the strength, courage and confidence to move on with my life. I learned the tools to overcome as many obstacles as possible so I could tell you my story.

One of my favourite people in the world and Energist, Silvia Hartmann, refers to our memories as data. It is just not there, it physically does not reside in your head. Take that old concept and paradigm out of your head!

Just bear in mind, most of the things we are told in our early years are fear and stress-based. People and society do their very best to condition us… (and keep us trapped, imprisoned and fearful!).

I remember watching one video by Tony Robbins. He was talking to a lady about her limiting beliefs, which she described as carrying around with her as baggage. He asked her if she was physically carrying that around with her, to which she replied: "No." At that moment she realised she had the option to continue to think about her "limiting beliefs" as her baggage or move on. Thankfully she did the latter.

At this point I would like you to imagine all the negatives there are in your life.

Here is a short list, just in case:

- Anxiety,
- Fear,
- Hurt,
- Depression,
- Rejection,
- Feeling unloved,
- Feeling unwanted,
- Feeling worthless,
- Unhappy,
- Underachieved,
- Lonely,
- Alone,
- Broke,
- Feeling stupid,

- Ugly,
- Low self-esteem,
- Not good enough,
- Guilty,
- Apprehensive,
- Scared,
- Traumatised,
- Dead inside,
- Etc. etc. etc.

Feel free to add as many more negatives as you wish - please be my guest.

Now imagine you have a rucksack, or if you want to (which I strongly suggest you do) think of each one of these negative emotions as a 1Kg book. All of these go in that rucksack, and you carry it with you wherever you go - up and down the stairs, first thing in the morning, late at night, when you go for a walk, when you are cycling, when you go for grocery shopping, when you see a friend. You cannot take it off.

How would you feel?

Tired?

In pain?

Losing the will to live?

Would you be happy to carry that rucksack (or burden, if you want to be more specific) each second of the day, for the rest of your life?

Would that be comfortable? Would others around you benefit at all? How much longer would you be willing to carry that rucksack with you?

Well, let me tell you, that rucksack is my metaphor for our limiting beliefs. We carry it constantly, all hours of the day, when we go to work, when we have lunch, etc. etc. etc.

If we were carrying a real rucksack, wouldn't it be fair to say that when you get tired of it, you make the decision to take it off? (There is that word again, "decision," and her sister's choice, option).

I would… In fact, I did get rid of that "imaginary" rucksack. Would you like to know more of how I did it?

I will share more with you in a minute, in my story section.

At this moment I would like to share with you a story a colleague and fellow trainer shared with some of us at a seminar in Bristol, England.

"We were having a conversation over a drink, just before dinner. My curious mind decided to raise the subject why some people hit rock bottom and then bounce back and others just don't!

Again my curiosity got the best/most of me.

She looked at me and smiled. She then looked at the rest of the trainers at the table and she started telling us a story she once heard.

In her very strong Portuguese accent she said: "There is a word, that word is called Decision. So a decision is when you make an incision in the mind, to cut free and away from what you don't want."

Here is the definition of Decision and Decide, according to The Oxford Dictionary.

> *Decision, (n) a conclusion or resolution reached after consideration.*
>
> *Decide, (v) come to or bring to a resolution in the mind as a result of consideration. – Origin ME: from Fr. Décider, from L. decider 'determine', from de- 'off' + caedere 'cut'.*

When I heard those words from Paola's mouth, I felt an extreme desire to find out even more what makes someone come to a resolution and cut free from their limiting beliefs, fears, stress, etc."

For now, let's look at how much it has cost you so far carrying that metaphorical rucksack? Have you achieved the results you wanted? Are people avoiding you? Are you a radiator or an extractor? What is your inner talk saying to you right now?

Please, take a few seconds (it doesn't take that long), and listen to your internal dialogue. What is it saying? About you? To you?

The more you hold on to the past, the longer it takes you to evolve it, change it or transform it. Notice I have not used that "c" word, "change"!

There is a book that illustrates what happens when we change nothing in our lives. We follow in the steps of our parents and forefathers. This book is '100 Years of Solitude' by Gabriel Garcia Marquez. Here he depicts three generations in one family and how cyclical their lives are, one generation doing the exact same thing as the previous one did, and making the same mistakes.

Is this your case?

I challenge you to take a look at your current life and map it over your parents' lives. Are there any similarities, or none at all? I can tell you from my personal experience I see more and more of my parents' behaviours each day, and that is after all the personal development work I have done, not having lived with them for over a decade. That's how powerful our parents' influencing is.

Do you like that overlap of careers, personalities and behaviours? Are they happy? (Your parents?)

What can you do to stop that spinning wheel and start living your life? And by YOUR life, I mean the life you have taken control of - made the choices and decisions to get you from A to F, and from D to M, without influencing, guilt or self-sabotage and owning all the consequences.

When you heal the past (which, I just remembered, I haven't told you yet how I did it) you let go of old and useless paradigms.

You become the person you always wanted to be, you start dreaming again, you see love and life everywhere, you experience a rebirth, you see solutions where you once saw problems.

People start gravitating toward you. You discover a sense and purpose in life, and you give it your all.

So, here is what I did to heal the past.

1. I made the decision I wanted to live a prosperous and abundant life. I recognised I was worth something in life. Just because I was born in poverty did not mean I had to stay poor forever.
2. I was honest with myself. This was one of the hardest things I ever did. To have the balls to say to yourself: "I messed up and this is the result of that," was not easy at all. I learned that owning my actions was the best tool I could ever utilise, so when anything happened I could look at it and prevent myself from making the same mistakes. At the same time I found I was giving myself some credit or all of the credit for when something went right. How many times or how often do you give yourself a pat on the back? When you are honest with yourself, you can do that. There is no dwelling in the past for anything. You embrace each day as if everything was a lesson to be learned.
3. I said yes to learning. I found that learning, which is very different to studying, was that missing link in my growth as an individual. I would read books about self-development and make the techniques and practices my own. Again, that curiosity we touched on earlier opens new doors to learning. I would talk to people with experience in that field or find ways to learn from someone who knew more about it than I did. I would watch TV programmes where people would talk about personal issues and there would be a panel of experts sharing their knowledge and expertise to really help them to evolve their "issues." I found that talking with a curious mind gave me many answers I was consciously looking for and those I was not consciously looking for too.
4. I opened my heart. When I opened my heart I was able to see the real beauty that lived in me. I didn't need any external validation because I was able to see it for myself. I grew and learned to love myself. I remember having a conversation with my mother one day, and she said to me: "Son, no one taught me how to love!" I was surprised, shocked and saddened by it. Our experiences in life were different and we too made different choices. I chose to learn to love myself first (yes, I always put myself first!), then use that new learned skill and love others. No one taught me to do this. I found out by myself, because of my curious mind!
5. I sought professional help. This was the icing on the cake. It had to happen for me to be able to really make that progression toward what I wanted in life. We are not supposed to be alone, we crave interaction with others (at least I do!). There is this magic that takes place when you speak to a professional. You break that chain of being a victim and you say: "I want help and I want a better life." I found that talking alone was all I needed. Knowing that someone was there to listen to me and offer me their support was enough to allow this paradigm shift to take place. When I spoke to

someone about my situation, it made me feel empowered and in control because I was able to see that I was doing something about it. It was the very first step I needed to make things happen. It isn't everyone's cup of tea - it just works.

Now I can tell you in more detail how I healed my past.

Healing The Past: My Story

Although you have already read some of the little things I did to heal my past, there is so much more.

When I made the decision to be better and add value in my life and into the lives of others, and enhanced that curiosity, I started seeing myself whole and complete.

I knew that to heal my past I had to let go of it. The shame, anger, fear and guilt were part of most of my teenage years. It was not going to be easy but it had to be done.

So, when the process began, I remember a particular memory, when one of my classmates from high school sat on my chair and read what I used to write on the back of my notebooks.

God, why me?

God, why me?

God, why me?

Does it sound familiar?

I had carried that burden for 13 years by then. It was part of my life and me. I saw it as my identity. I was all of those things - I was shame, I was anger, I was fear, I was guilt and many other negative things.

Remembering that particular incident gave me the courage to close that door and focus on what mattered, my now, and start looking forward to the future.

As I already mentioned, I firstly made the decision to be better, followed by the decision of wanting a prosperous and abundant life. I did not know what that was when I decided that was what I wanted, but I was willing to find out.

I became even more curious about those who had achieved what I wanted, which fed my curiosity. When you are curious as to what is happening in your head or your heart, you start getting to know yourself even more. Or if you didn't know yourself in the first place, guess what? You grow and learn to know yourself.

This knowledge then became mastery. I mastered my life, I was in control, I had the reins for once – oh, and how encouraging that was. I was always a good boy, I did as I was told. I was conditioned and that was all I knew.

When I healed my past, I cut that umbilical cord that had me attached to it. I gained control of my emotions, my heart, my soul and my life.

Isn't this what we all deserve?

When I was stuck in the past, in the old boy being good, I had no voice, no opinion, no choice, and yes, you probably guessed it, NO LIFE.

Thank God for curiosity. Although I have said it before, I will stress it again… CURIOSITY is the spark that lights your life. I learned so much through curiosity, I still do. I look at the world as if it were my first day in it.

I want to know more about animals, plants, spirituality, people and even you, although I haven't met you yet.

If I didn't let go of unwanted beliefs and behaviours, I realised I would stay imprisoned in my own imaginary prison for the rest of my life.

I had this image of me in this small prison cell, eating rotten carcasses, drinking from a contaminated well, crying my eyes out, skin and bones, wishing life was better, looking at the greener grass outside of my cell, growing lonely and old, not realising the key to open that gate was there all along. I just could not see it.

The second I had that image, I stepped into the cell, shook him up and said to him (myself): "There is the key, it has been there all along. Open it and enjoy your life."

It felt so good, to know that I had an endless supply of plasters to heal that past. And I would like to stress and clarify, not for one second did I want to pretend things never happened. On the contrary, I wanted to acknowledge them and take ownership, by saying out loud: "You have happened and I am in control. You do not rule my life, I have the reins of my destiny."

Now, you do it. Say out loud:

"You have happened and I am in control. You do not rule my life, I have the reins of my destiny.

You have happened and I am in control. You do not rule my life, I have the reins of my destiny.

You have happened and I am in control. You do not rule my life, I have the reins of my destiny."

Stand in front of a mirror and say it even louder, looking at yourself in the eyes.

The moment I felt that freedom flowing through me, I knew I had let go of those memories and negativity. I knew from that moment on that, whatever came my way, I was in control… Yes, there have been many rocking moments in my life since that decision was made. Yes, I have felt out of control. Yes, I have said: "Come on, not again!" It is normal to react like that. What matters is what happens next. Will you carry that with you for the next two decades, put it in a cosy corner of your imaginary rucksack? Or will you say to yourself: "You know what, I messed it up and it is OK. Let's move on, but before we move on, let's see what we can improve or learn from this."?

Then came this explosion of love. I didn't know what had happened at the time, I just felt compassion toward everyone. I wanted to really make a difference and empower others so they too could experience what I had.

This love allowed me to explore more what I had been through and contrast it with other people's experiences - to seek patterns and commonalities so I could speak a universal truth that resonated with everyone. This includes you too!

At this stage of my former years, I had broken away from my past. Yet there were some "niggles" there I still had to deal with. This is when I sought professional help. As mentioned previously, I did the talk therapies, took the drugs, but they didn't go to the core of what I wanted to work on. That came later.

Although I will talk about them in a moment, the therapies/techniques I used to help me move in the right direction were NLP (Neuro Linguistic Programming), EFT (Emotional Freedom Techniques), Modern Stress Management, Coaching, Reiki, Crystal Healing, Project Sanctuary and Energy Work.

I did find group therapy highly useful. We took our masks off and shared with other people our most intimate concerns and, led by a psychologist, it would be the participants who would come up with the solutions. Very powerful indeed! I learned my life was slightly better than others, and worse than some too. I had the opportunity to not only learn from my mistakes and past but that of others too.

This eventually led me to want to learn more about human behaviour and communication. I took this as my opportunity to really go to the root of my beliefs and programming - ultimately to really and fully understand how I operated as an individual and help others to also understand their programming and learn how to evolve their lives to new horizons and possibilities.

The skills I learned were (and please let me advise you, you needn't go to this extent to develop the skills to get to know yourself) coaching, asking powerful questions to make me analyse, deconstruct situations and come up with the answers myself.

I also learned: leadership and management; NLP, Neuro-Linguistic Programming, which I read about when I was 15 years old, applied psychology to help you get from where you are to where you want to be; Reiki, to nurture my spirituality. Here I learned about energy which ultimately led me to EFT, Emotional Freedom Techniques - using the meridian centres of the body, where the energy becomes trapped and can lead to negative emotions and/or even pains and aches. It is like acupuncture without needles. The understanding of all of these techniques took me to a deeper level of appreciation of how we as humans operate.

So, I took the learning of these skills as an opportunity to further work on my "issues and problems," as we will have "stuff" to work on regularly. It was also an opportunity to gain a qualification to show, teach and empower others how to take control of their lives in the now and heal the past, effortlessly, in control and, guess what, in a fun manner.

Letting go of the past and healing it needn't be dull or painful.

I have shared this with you, and you may even be thinking by now… Wow... This all I needed. Then great, as long you as you choose to be better and add value to the world, are curious and heal the past - fantastic. These three things alone will give you enough energy to build into your confidence.

Just imagine what you will know by the end of Step 10!

Healing The Past: Things To Avoid

When you start exploring past memories, traumas, events etc., you must ensure you do it from a place of control.

If you start reliving the memory all over again, crying your eyes out, shaking and feeling like a "victim," do you think you are in control?

Can you honestly get any sort of resolution when you are still affected by it?

The answer is quite simple: NO.

Healing the past needn't mean you have to go back to that feeling of hurt, powerlessness, upset, etc..

The real secret is to remember you are in control, and that whatever it is you are working on, it's long gone.

IT CAN NOT HURT YOU, OR HAPPEN AGAIN.

By no means would this show you are denying it happened. On the contrary, you are saying: "It happened, it is not affecting me, so what? Bring it on!"

I would like to give you an example, another one of my analogies.

Imagine you are watching a horror film, and the most disgusting and horrible and creepy creature you have ever seen appears on the screen. Would you be upset and cry, because it "looks" scary or would you remain tranquil and serene?

It is only a movie, it cannot come off the screen and hurt you, or can it? Or is it just your imagination playing tricks on you?

What you can do to prevent this feeling is endless. You can switch the TV off, go to a different room, watch another programme, etc. etc. etc...

Working with memories from the past is no different.

Just bear it in mind.

Healing The Past: The Exercises

What exercises can I come up with? I am asking myself and you too are probably asking yourself!

You needn't worry, I will be gentle.

1. Past Memory

Take one memory, ideally one that wasn't that strong and has no control over you in the present.

I would like you to replay that memory in your mind's eye, with your eyes closed, from the beginning to the end.

What do you notice? Who is there? What are you doing? What day of the week is it? What time of the day is it? Time of the year? What happens?

Remember, you are in control of this memory. If you find yourself reliving the memory and you get upset, open your eyes if necessary.

Notice the colours, sounds and feelings. Are they vivid colours? Loud and banging sounds? Strong negative feelings?

Is there someone involved there too?

Who is this person? Do you know them? Or are they strangers?

Go through that memory several times, as if it were a movie, or an episode in a movie.

When you have done it enough -

Open your eyes, and shake it all off. Get up and dance if you can.

Now go to the climax of that memory. Once you are there, I would like you to change the colours, make them brighter and funkier. If there were people involved, change their voices, make them really squeaky and funny and then shrink them to the size of an ant, and even smaller and smaller until they disappear.

Once you have done this, just change the rest of the scenery. Bring new objects, people, whatever you want to bring in, and see what happens. At the end try in vain to remember that memory, and see how you feel about it.

If you find there is some intensity left there, do it again, and again and again, until there is no charge left there.

After you have done this with minor, small memories, move onto the more heavy duty ones. Repeat the same steps, until there is no intensity and charge left in that memory.

Remember, you are in control. You can always open your eyes at any moment and resume when you feel more relaxed. Do not forget my analogy of the horror film. There is a myriad of things you can do to not let the memory affect you.

2. Different Angles To A Problem

This exercise derives from an NLP, Neuro-Linguistic Programming, technique called perceptual positions.

Take a situation in which you and somebody else have been involved in the past. It doesn't matter how long ago it took place.

You can do this exercise sitting down or standing up in the same place. You can mark some specific areas on the floor. You can do it with your eyes open or closed. The option is yours.

Look at this situation through your eyes.

What did you see? What did you feel? What did you hear? What did you smell? What did you taste? What was your internal dialogue like? What are you thinking?

Play this scenario, hear the words the other person said. What did you both say? What was the location where this took place?

Once you have played this memory, shake it all off. Get up, walk, let the energy be released.

At this point you can repeat this part of the exercise, to make sure you didn't miss anything out.

When you are 100% satisfied, you can move on to the next step.

Look at the situation through the other person's eyes.

What did they see? What did they feel? What did they hear? What did they smell? What did they taste? What was their internal dialogue like? What are they thinking?

Is there anything you have discovered here, now that you have looked at their side of the story?

Play this scenario, hear their words, hear what you said. What did you both say? What was the location where this took place? Is the location the same or has it changed?

Once you have played this memory, shake it all off. Get up, walk, let the energy be released.

At this point you can repeat this part of the exercise, to make sure you didn't miss anything out.

When you are 100% satisfied you can move onto the next step.

Now, I invite you to look at the situation from an outsider's point of view - or as a fly on the wall, as it were. Whatever works for you.

What is this person seeing? Is this person seeing the same as the other two?

What is this person hearing? Is this person hearing the same story as the other two?

What is this person feeling? Is this person feeling the same as the other two?

If there was any advice this person or fly on the wall could give them, what would it be?

What advice would this person give you?

Take a moment and listen to it. Then receive that advice.

What advice would this person give to the other person?

Take a moment and listen to it. Then let the other person receive that advice too.

When you have completed this part of the exercise, as before, get up and shake it all off, let the energy flow.

Now, I would invite you to visit those three spaces again.

Firstly, look at that situation from your own eyes, after having seen the other person's side and the third person's too. Has the situation changed? Have your feelings about it changed too? What are your feeling towards the other person? What are your thoughts now?

Explore the memory and, when you are ready, step out and shake it off.

Now, visit the situation from the other person's point of view. Has it changed? Have their feelings about this situation changed? What are their feelings towards you? What are their thoughts now?

Explore the memory and, when you are ready, step out and shake it off.

Lastly, visit the memory from the outsider's point of view. How do they see this situation now? Have they come to any form of resolution? Is there any work left to be done? What words of wisdom or final advice can s/he give to them so they can evolve this situation and move forward?

When you have explored this memory, situation from all three points of view, come out of it and shake it off, let the energy flow.

Repeat this exercise as many times as you feel it is needed. You can work on the same memory multiple times. In fact, I encourage you to do so. This would determine how much the memory and your feelings about it have evolved.

Write any insights or lessons you have taken from it.

Now, imagine yourself in a similar situation in the future. How would you react? What would you do differently? Most importantly, how do you see that other person now?

Like before, use this exercise on minor memories. Use it as often as you can, daily if possible. The more comfortable you become with this exercise, the better it is for you to explore stronger memories and look at it from different perspectives, so you can evolve your past memories and heal the past to create the life you know you deserve.

Note any discoveries, notes, insights or lessons. I strongly suggest you write them down in your journal, which by now should be a few pages long.

3. The Sweetest Words: I Love You

I would like you to image a very painful and/or hurtful memory (without getting too associated into it).

Firstly I invite you to play it in your mind's eye, just the way it happened originally… If you do get upset, stand up and shake it all off.

Then, rather than hearing those hurtful and painful words, I would like to change all the negative and upsetting words for I Love Yous.

For example,

My aunty shouted at me, you are a very bad boy.

I would change it to,

My aunty lovingly said to me, I Love You.

Feel the difference in yourself and notice how the memory changes and with it your feelings about it.

Remember, the only thing that could or in fact will hinder you is your imagination, be as creative as you possibly can and heal those past wounds with many I Love Yous.

In fact, I DO Love you.

Goodbye, Farewell ...

Broken, half alive I lived a life I was not proud of.
I lived in the past and the memories,
Yet, nothing was done.
I tried to let go, but my fears of losing my identity
Betrayed me and I became a prisoner.
Please save me, please save me,
Said the inner voice, said the child.
I had done all I could to let go of yesterday,
The pain is just too strong,
I want to move on but what do I do?
I have asked this question many times.
Do I sleep and hope it goes away,
I thought I have tried and I know it doesn't work.
The land of the free says the TV.
Is there freedom where I am?
I am a prisoner! I have been lied to!
I want to be free, once more, what do I do?
I want to let go, I just don't know how.
I think of the past and pain comes back.
I want to be free, I want to be me.
Cured and healed, sane once more.
I look at my former self in the eye and say:
You! Let me go, I don't want to be your prisoner any more.
You! Listen and listen well, I don't want you near me,
Just go, and take my pain with you.
I have suffered long because of you,
You don't serve me any more, I don't need you.
I want to move forward and enjoy my life once more.
Let go, let go, let go of me.
I forgive you, I set you free.
Now the time is right, the time is now,
Goodbye, farewell, I set myself free,
Goodbye, farewell, now I start to live,
Goodbye, farewell, now I can be.

Step 4: Learning from the Past

"People spend too much time finding other people to blame, too much energy finding excuses for not being what they are capable of being, and not enough energy putting themselves on the line, growing out of the past, and getting on with their lives."

J. Michael Straczynski

This section is designed as a tool to encourage learning from past memories, events and situations, so we have a richer set of skills we can use as point of reference to view the present and the future.

Although I have covered some of this in the previous chapters, there are some other elements we can add when we heal the past.

I have mentioned journaling in Steps 1, 2 and 3. There are countless ways in which you can use a journal. I personally have 8 different journals. I promise you it isn't as scary as it may sound.

I use to record different things, so this is what I used them for:

- Ideas journal: here I record any idea I have during the day. I also write quotes or anything of interest.
- A thought, behaviour tracker journal: I use this journal to capture what happens in my head throughout the day, any negative self-talk or "strange" behaviours, so I can explore them later.
- Wants and wish journal: I like putting in writing things I would like to get, so I can then evaluate whether they are really that important, urgent, vital and whether by obtaining them my life may be enriched.

The next 3 journals stem from a process designed by one of my mentors, John Seymour, called Personal Evolution Process or PEP.

- Daily journal: here you review the main elements of the last 24 hours.
- Learning log journal: here you write down what you have learned from the last 24 hours, what worked, what didn't work, what can be improved, etc.
- Personal evolution outcomes journal: what you want to do for the next day and what you are going to do differently as a result of what you have learned.
- Gratitude journal: here I like to highlight things I am grateful for, like health, food, friends, family etc.
- Dream journal (some other people call it dream books, I prefer the word journal): during the night when we dream our unconscious mind talks to us through metaphors, dreams and images. By keeping a log of what you dream, you are able to look for patterns, commonalities, messages, etc.

I know I have been stressing journaling before - I just cannot stress it enough.

Journaling is a good way of keeping track of your thoughts and ideas. It can be used as an idea generator, allows you to become more creative, and you can visit it at any time, see what was happening in your life, in your head, a week, month or year earlier.

Isn't it worth your while exploring what is happening in your life and seeing what impact, be it positive or negative, these actions/thoughts or ideas can have in it?

In his book 'The Slight Edge,' Jeff Olson talks about the small actions/activities we do on a daily basis and how they will have a significant impact in our future. We may not be able to see them immediately, but in 3, 5, 10 years we will see them. This goes in alignment with the compounded effect. Those small steps we take today, together they compound and create a bigger step which gets us closer to our goals and wants in life.

So by journaling, we are able to look at our past and see what went on, through our own words, so then we can find solutions and evolve it.

Another tool I find highly effective when learning from the past is to speak to people about my past, especially those who were there, with whom I created those memories.

Obviously, I encourage you to act with caution when you talk to people about the past, especially if you are talking about a negative incident.

When you speak to the other person about a specific memory, you are able to discuss what went on, how you both felt about it, what impact it had in your lives. Another word of advice - put your emotions to one side.

Talking to people who were involved in a positive or negative memory with you, you can both take the exercise you did in step 3, perceptual positions, making it more real. Both parties can talk honestly and openly and learn from their past.

Watching home movies is yet another great way of learning from your former self. If you were fortunate enough to have recorded anniversaries, Christmases, birthdays, holidays etc., I invite you to play them and watch yourself.

- What were you doing? Do you remember the day? Were you happy or sad? What were you celebrating?
- What do you think the former you could have done differently?
- Did anything happen before or after that video was filmed?
- What lessons can you take by watching that video?
- Do you remember what you wanted to do and achieve when you were that age? Have you accomplished those things?
- The people in the video - how is your relationship with them? Compared to then? If you aren't talking to them, what has happened? What could you have done differently?

You see how by journaling, talking to people and watching videos of ourselves we can take lessons and bring them to the present, not only to heal the past, but to improve the present and make the future even better.

Learning From The Past: My Story

I understand that when you are doing your best to move on and let go of the past, looking for lessons may seem crazy and pointless. You just want that magical band aid that will make it go away. Then in the years to come, if we remember, we will consider taking the time, courage and energy to revisit that memory and "try" to find any lessons.

Well, here is my story and how I benefited by learning from the past.

I believe that by now you may have noticed I am not any different to any of you. I had a turbulent past, I felt there was no point, I had doubts, very low self-esteem, I had no self-worth, I was a prisoner in my own body. In fact, I have made many mistakes - still make them. I am guilty of that!

What I found ever so beneficial was to dissociate myself from the past. As I have said before, not pretending it didn't exist, but to empower myself and take the control from the past and put it in my hands in the now.

After having complained about my life, like we all do, I looked back to my past with a new pair of glasses. Let's call them the "kindness glasses."

I looked at my past and all of the events that took place between my birth and when I decided to be gentler with myself and noticed many positive things:

- I was looked after by my family,
- I had good food,
- I was sent to school,
- I had good heath,
- I had a roof over my head,
- I was given nice things (which I didn't know at the time, how much my parents had to sacrifice),
- I had good water to drink,
- I was loved,
- I had all the reasons in the world to be grateful for my life.

When I put that into perspective, I thought to myself: "Who am I to forget all the wonderful things I had as a child or teenager and only focus on the negative?"

What good comes out of looking at my life through dirty and distorted lenses?

Yes, I cried. Yes, things happened to me. Yes, my parents shouted at me. Yes, my neighbours and peers picked on me.

But why should I let that define me? Keep me trapped and under their control?

The past taught me that if you focus on the negative, you will get more of that. At the same time if you focus on the good and positive things in life, guess what, those things will come to your life.

So, I stopped focusing on anything that wasn't good about my past and I remembered all the incredible things I had.

I was born in the Tropics. My goodness, I hear people saving to move to where I was born. Mustn't have been that bad if people want to live where I was born.

I had the freshest of fruit and vegetables, straight from the tree. It doesn't get any better than that.

I had toys, I had potable water, I had electricity, I had a comfortable bed.

How bad was that!

I can feel this sense of embarrassment coming over me, to type all the things I had, when I know there are millions of people worse off than I was, and they do not complain about their lives the way I did. They look forward to the next day, with hope in their hearts and the dream that life will be better.

I had nothing to look forward to, because I took my whole childhood and teenage years for granted. I learned that I took my sibling and parents for granted and many others along the way.

I was sent to school… What a horrible thing to do to a child! I was being invested in… My goodness, it doesn't get any worse than that! Or does it?

These are some of the things I learned from my past - that what I have now is the result of my efforts (and my parents too, obviously!), and at the same time that there are people who would love to have what I had as a child.

When I read and hear the news, I feel a knot in my throat. To even consider making a comment about sadness and injustice in my life doesn't compare to what some people go through in life day in and day out.

Do they complain?

Do we hear them moan and groan?

No we don't, because their hope is in the future.

The past for them is a mirage that is there, but they would much rather focus on what there is to come, their future and more life!

Now, whenever anything goes wrong in my life, I dwell on it for 2 seconds, take the lessons I can from it and move on, as quickly as I can.

This is what I have learned from the past - there is no point, the only thing that matters is the now, the moment, the present.

Some say: "They call it the present because it is that - a present to us."

Are you willing to honour that present? Share with others and make a difference in the world?

I AM. I am doing it right now!

Looking at the past and learning from it needn't be painful. I encourage you to do it and when you feel nostalgic or upset, look at the lives of millions of people who would like to be in your position.

How would you feel then?

So far we have learned 4 simple, yet powerful steps to Grow Confident: choosing to be better and adding value, being curious, healing the past and now learning from the past.

How much more do you need to learn to Grow even more Confident?

Learning From The Past: Things To Avoid

I urge you to only focus on the positive lessons. In fact, there are no negative lessons.

Just focus on what can make a difference to you in your life right now, on something that is going to empower you and propel you to move forward.

When you visit the past, you needn't dwell on it. Find a strategy that will allow you to visit a memory, get the lessons from it and move on.

If you find yourself getting upset every time you visit a memory, then there is some work to be done. Remember, there are professionals out there willing to help you.

I am against comparing oneself to others. Though when you find yourself feeling sorry for yourself and your past, watch the news and compare your past to theirs.

See how they smile to the cameras and look at the hope in their eyes.

Learning From The Past: The Exercises

In order to learn from the past, you must want to learn to evolve and move forward. I have already mentioned you can do the exercise from the previous step, perceptual positions. I also mentioned watching videos, reading your journals or diaries, talking to people, etc.

Before I move on to the exercises, there is a really great NLP technique called Time Line. I strongly suggest you look it up and try it for yourself. This is a great tool to heal the past and get those lessons from it.

1. The List Of Lessons

I would like you to make an honest list of what lessons you have learned in the last decade or so, from a past event or memory, which was significant enough in your life.

It is important that you are 100% honest. No-one needs to see this. It is personal and private, only you have access to it. Again, please write it in your journal. By now you may have seen how valuable a tool it can be and will be in your future. Always date it and sign it, make it your friend.

1. ______________________________
2. ______________________________
3. ______________________________
4. ______________________________
5. ______________________________
6. ______________________________
7. ______________________________
8. ______________________________
9. ______________________________
10. ______________________________

Once you have written them down, put them to one side. Please do not read them straight away.

A day or so later, take your journal out and read the lessons. Have you seen the benefits of having learned what you learned? Is there anything else you would like to add to those lessons?

How differently will you react when you find yourself facing a similar event? Will you remember your lessons?

Do this with one, two, three events and memories. Or if you feel courageous enough, do it with all the memories you can think of, even positive ones.

Can you see how learning from the past has the potential to make you Grow Confident?

You have made the mistakes, learned what you had to from it, now you are ready for whatever is thrown at you.

Don't you find this powerful in itself?

2. Missing Lessons

You know yourself better than most people, and more than you give yourself credit for.

Take a look at your life and make an honest list of what you haven't learned, that by learning your life would be even better.

Let me make myself clearer. What have you not learned that can be of great benefit in your life right now?

Make a list of all the things you haven't learned that you know by learning now would be of benefit.

This list can be as long or as short as you wish, though I suggest you write a minimum of 10 lessons in this list.

1. ______________________________
2. ______________________________
3. ______________________________
4. ______________________________
5. ______________________________
6. ______________________________
7. ______________________________
8. ______________________________
9. ______________________________
10. ______________________________

Just as before, put them to one side for a day or two, then revisit them. Is there anything else you would like to add to this list?

Make any required amendments.

When you are ready, next to each one of these missing lessons, I invite you to write the memory where you think you should have learned it from.

It can be more than one memory. Sometimes we need to be reminded of lessons many times before we remember them.

1. ____
2. ____
3. ____
4. ____
5. ____
6. ____
7. ____
8. ____
9. ____
10. ____

When you finish, as before, put them to one side for a day or two. Take these "missing lessons" and memories out and add any you may have forgotten.

Read them one by one, out loud if you wish. Do it once.

Then I invite you to read them for a second time. As you do this, I encourage you to take that learning into your body and keep it there. How does it feel? Can you hear or see anything?

Do this with all the memories, one by one. When you come to the last one, I welcome you to imagine future events when these new lessons may come in handy.

Please, do not forget to write these down in your journal.

3. Knowledge & Skills

Although what we do and know does not define us, in this next exercise I would like you to make a list of all the skills and knowledge you have gained throughout your life.

Please, just as before, honesty first.

1. ____
2. ____
3. ____
4. ____
5. ____
6. ____
7. ____
8. ____
9. ____
10. ____

The idea of this exercise is to remind you of what you have achieved in your life so far, and also to prove that knowledge from the past is of use and beneficial to you. You only need to be shown how to channel it and use it to your advantage.

Learn And Be Free

I used to study, very little I did learn.
I went through life aimlessly,
I rose up, I got up, I worked, I ate and I slept.
I was a robot, a machine programmed to get by.
Little did I know, this was my life.
And then… one day something changed.
I rose up and I was not the same.
I heard this voice loud and clear,
Clear and loud this voice was,
What have you learned so far, my dear boy?
Learned? I inquired back.
There is no such thing as learning, I replied.
We go to school to study, it is the only way,
No options, no alternatives.
I grew and I studied, I studied as I grew.
Nonsense, said the now angry voice,
To be, to have and to do, learn you must,
Master all that you can learn,
Master and learn from your emotions,
Master and learn from yourself,
Master and learn from the past.
You see, my dear boy, real men learn,
But learning isn't what you think,
Learning is to understand what has happened,
Learning is to break away from paradigms,
Learning is when you accept who you are,
No criticism, no attachment.
When you learn you are,
When you learn you can be,
When you learn you know that you know
My child, my dear boy, wake up, wake up.
Learn and master, master and learn,
Let go, move on, learn and be free.

Step 5: Modelling

"Modelling is an incredible platform."

Cameron Russell

In this step I will talk to you about an NLP, Neuro-Linguistic Programming, technique called modelling, which will help you understand how successful people do what they do. Or, in our case, model someone's confidence, so we are able to respond and react the way these people would do and get similar results.

For those of you who aren't familiar with NLP, I highly recommend that you take a look at it. It was the very first personal development art I learned about as a teenager, when it had been around for only two decades. Now, four decades on, the amount of information on it is so vast that you are spoiled for choice.

Some good sources to find out more are www.youtube.com where you can watch videos on techniques and see some of the biggest names in NLP doing what they do best. There are numerous books on NLP and there is also an encyclopaedia of NLP by Robert Dilts and Judith DeLozier.

As I have mentioned previously, I believed in what NLP could do – for I have seen many incredible results using it, to the point that I became a master practitioner and trainer of NLP. Not that you have to go to that extent - just inform yourself enough and take from it what you feel is needed.

With all this being said, let's get started with what modelling is.

The following is an extract from the Encyclopaedia of Systemic Neuro-Linguistic Programming and NLP New Coding, Robert Dilts and Judith DeLozier, 2000, NLP University Press.

> *Modelling: Webster's Dictionary defines a model as "a simplified description of a complex entity or process" – such as a "computer model" of the circulatory and respiratory systems. The term comes from the Latin root modus, which means "a manner of doing or being; a method, form, fashion, custom, way, or style." More specifically, the word "model" is derived from the Latin modulus, which essentially means a "small" version of the original mode. A "model" of an object, for example, is typically a miniature version or representation of that object.*
>
> *A "working model" (such as that of a machine) is something which can do on a small scale the work which the machine itself does, or is expected to do. From this perspective, the fundamental value of any type of model is its usefulness.*

Now that we have the most accurate definition of modelling, let's explore how it can work for us.

When you want to model a behaviour, attitude or technique, it is key and paramount that you choose a person or number of people you feel comfortable modelling, someone you resonate with, and most importantly the most useful technique for you.

Once you identify who this person is, or people, watch them live or on video and take a look at:

- Body language,
- Breathing,
- Eyes,
- Posture,
- Language used,
- Any noticeable mannerism,
- Environment - where are they at their best?
- Who is around them?
- Time of the day,
- Season of the year,
- Any hidden patterns?

After you make a list of the above mentioned qualities, if you are in a position to personally talk to the person, either face to face or on the phone, ask the following questions:

- What are they thinking about when they do what they do?
- Are they conscious of their movements?
- Do they have a ritual before or during what they do?
- Do they use visualisation skills?
- Have they got a lucky charm?
- How much training do they do?
- How many hours do they spend doing what they do?
- What makes them so good at what they do?

You may notice that at times they may be unaware of what they do, and that is OK. Learn what you can from them.

How does this relate to Growing Confident?

If you know of someone who is very or extremely confident and you would like to model that, you can use the above questions and observations to gain information on what makes them so confident in contrast to other people. And by doing this you are creating, or rather modelling, their confidence strategy.

I like to look at modelling as borrowing someone's belief system and embracing it until we are able to create our own belief system about x, y or z.

To be even more precise, what we are doing is learning through somebody else's experience.

If you aren't able to ask the person directly how they do their behaviours, what you can do is what we discussed previously in one of the exercises, which is using perceptual positions. By putting yourself in that person's shoes you can see, hear and feel what they see, hear and feel when doing what they do. Do not underestimate this skill - you can gain a lot of information if you allow yourself to.

Once you understand the basics of modelling, you can model absolutely anything you like. The only limit would be the one you put on yourself.

Just imagine for one second, that you skilfully learn to model someone's confidence to the point that you become very confident, bearing in mind that you are only adding to what you have already learned; choosing to be better, being curious, healing and learning from the past. How much better would your life look at this point?

Now, I would like to stress and highlight that what we know as "limiting beliefs," "obstacles," "barriers," "negative thoughts/patterns/behaviours" aren't that real at all… They are only data!!!

These concepts and ideas, to use the philosophy and lessons from one of my mentors Silvia Hartmann, are entities which we have created ourselves. So essentially we are responsible for these patterns, behaviours and thoughts we follow and allow to take control over us.

Once upon a time, some person took the decision to "name" things. These things or words were passed from one generation to the next and the next and the next, and so on and so forth, till they arrived at our doorstep.

What you and I are experiencing is just the aftermath or compounded effect of those "false beliefs," which have been made bigger and whose control over us has become even greater with time.

By modelling or borrowing someone's beliefs you are embracing that positive, empowering belief, a can-do attitude, and you are breaking away from old and useless paradigms that have held society and humanity back for centuries.

When you start modelling something for the first time, it may seem fake, strange, odd, unusual, but, like everything else, with time it just gets easier. At first it will feel a bit clunky and clumsy. Again, with time it becomes more second-nature and effortless, until it becomes more you.

We have heard time and time again: "Practice is the mother of all arts." Modelling is an art in itself. Why not become really good at it, until we become confident too?

Can you see yourself modelling a skill or a person in the future?

If so, what would it be?

Just imagine - what will it feel like?

Modelling: My Story

Although I wasn't too conscious about modelling when I was growing up, as I have mentioned a few times by now, I had this curiosity, so that I modelled people without realising what I was doing.

So, I would watch TV and look at the actors on the movies and soap operas and notice how they composed themselves and behaved. Then I would practise or pretend, which I think would be more accurate, and embody who they were.

I have to be honest and admit that it didn't help much as a child or teenager because I would just do it a minute or two and then forget about it. I didn't practise enough to be confident by doing it.

Based on that, I will be frank - I was rubbish at modelling. I was curious and I would model, but the repetition was lacking.

It wasn't until I discovered it by its proper and real name, later in my life, that modelling became a really useful tool.

Like many people, I had a fear of public speaking. Thankfully it is a lot better these days. This was holding me back and was not serving me in the slightest.

What I did was, I looked at people who were really good at public speaking - particularly people who did what I wanted to do, personal development.

I then became this "cyber-stalker." I watched as many videos as possible of the people I wanted to model.

I looked at their body language, and the language they used. I would look for any clues in their presenting skills.

The more videos I looked at, and the more focused I was on the details, the more I started to notice a strategy, a map, a route they all followed.

After I had this strategy, I would put it into practice and ask myself or people around me:

- How does this feel?
- Do I feel nervous?
- Do I look comfortable?
- Do I sound like them?
- Is there anything else missing?

Most importantly, I would compare and contrast people's styles and strategies and come up with my own.

This was perhaps the single most useful lesson from my modelling practices - making those models and strategies my own, putting my personality and signature on it.

I learned that because you model someone's *modus operandi* does not mean you have to be a copy-cat. We are all individuals, and the sole idea of learning a skill is to make it your own.

The amount of skills, attitudes and behaviours I have modelled is endless. I see that as honouring a person's talents and sharing these skills or knowledge with other people, so they too can benefit from it.

One last thing: I understood that modelling is part of us. We did everything as children by modelling those around us. We modelled our parents' mannerisms, we modelled people on TV, we modelled language, etc., etc., etc...

Why not let it work with us and for us?

Modelling: Things To Avoid

There is only one word of advice I would like to give you and that is to be original. Model until you become comfortable with what you want to learn. If it is confidence, model a person until you feel comfortable in your "own skin."

After you have played with modelling for a while, do your very best to make it your own, rather than being a real "copy-cat."

Another thing I would like to highlight is that just because you are modelling someone or some people, it does not mean that you are either an identity thief or that you don't have an identity of your own. On the contrary, it means that you value and care for your identity so that you are checking for yourself what there is out there that works and what doesn't work.

Do not listen to people's negative comments.

Remember at all times, you are modelling excellence to Grow Confident, so then you can go out into the world and add value to as many people as you possibly can.

Modelling: The Exercises

1. Find Your Strategies

I would like you to take a skill of your own and dissect it.

Find out: what is it you do that makes you really good at it?

Just like I illustrated earlier in the chapter, identify what your behaviours are and what is happening internally.

What is your …

- Body language,
- Breathing,
- Eyes,
- Posture,
- Language used,
- Any noticeable mannerism,
- Environment: where are you at your best?
- Who is around you?
- Time of the day,
- Season of the year,
- Any hidden patterns?

Ask yourself the following questions:

- What are you thinking about when you do what you do?
- Are you conscious of your movements?
- Do you have a ritual before or during what you do?
- Do you use visualisation skills?
- Have you got a lucky charm?
- How much training do you do?
- How many hours do you spend doing what you do?
- What makes you so good at what you do?

Once you have traced your pattern, or mapped it out, share it with someone and see how well they do it.

You may wish to show them first, especially if it is something physical, so they don't harm themselves. Or if it is something they do but not as well as you, see how much their results improve with your strategy.

Do it and impress others and yourself, and you will also be making a difference in someone's life by teaching them a new skill.

2. Model A Skill Or Technique

As mentioned earlier, one of the most effective ways of learning a skill is by observation and modelling.

Pick a person, or some people, you would like a skill or technique from. Just as before, look at their behaviours and either ask them the questions or second position yourself to answer these questions.

What is their …

- Body language,
- Breathing,
- Eyes,
- Posture,
- Language used,
- Any noticeable mannerism,
- Environment: where are they at their best?
- Who is around them?
- Time of the day,
- Season of the year,
- Any hidden patterns?

Ask them the following questions:

- What are they thinking about when they do what they do?
- Are they conscious of their movements?
- Do they have a ritual before or during what they do?
- Do they use visualisation skills?
- Have they got a lucky charm?
- How much training do they do?
- How many hours do they spend doing what they do?
- What makes them so good at what they do?

Once you have traced their pattern, or mapped it out, do it and see how well you do it. Please be careful and do not do anything extreme unless you are 100% comfortable, or supervised at least.

You may wish to show the person how you do their skill (if they are nearby), especially if it is something physical, so they can correct you if needed. Get their feedback. If it is something you had done before, how much have your results improved with your new strategy? Does it need improving?

Remember, the key to any modelling project is practice, practice, practice. You have the potential to be as good as anyone, so as long as you put in the hours of practice and commitment to reach that level of mastery.

3. Make A List

I invite you to make a list of a minimum of 30 skills or techniques you want to either improve on or learn.

The idea behind this exercise is to encourage you to gain new skills, which will build on to the ones you already have.

How much do you think this will enhance and increase your confidence? How much value will you add, not only to your life but to that of others too?

I also encourage you to give these skills a deadline you would like to learn them by. Write the name of the person you are going to model and why you want to learn or enhance that skill.

Skill	Deadline	Person to be modelled
1.		
2.		
3.		
4.		
5.		
6.		
7.		
8.		
9.		
10.		
11.		
12.		
13.		
14.		
15.		
16.		
17.		
18.		
19.		
20.		
21.		
22.		

23.		
24.		
25.		
26.		
27.		
28.		
29.		
30.		

You needn't fill in every row in this box today, there is no pressure whatsoever. Though I do encourage you to be as imaginative and adventurous as possible with the skills you want to learn. You never know, you may find you learn more than 30 skills in one or two years, and then learn more and more, until you grow to a new dimension and the value you add is beyond what you ever imagined you could add to the lives of people around you.

Note: write the skills and techniques you want to learn in your journal.

4. Modelling A Confident Person

Just in case you thought you were going to get away with not modelling a person - sorry, this is your next exercise.

I encourage you to pick a person you know and you can talk to, either on the phone or face to face.

Explain the nature of the exercise. They will thank you for choosing them as your model - and isn't it a great compliment to them too?

As before, dissect and analyse what they do and how they do it. Ask them to be patient with you in advance, so neither of you feel uncomfortable during the process.

What is their …

- Body language,
- Breathing,
- Eyes,
- Posture,
- Language used,
- Any noticeable mannerism,
- Environment: where are they at their best?
- Who is around them?
- Time of the day,
- Season of the year,
- Any hidden patterns?

Ask them the following questions:

- What are they thinking about when they do what they do?
- Are they conscious of their movements?
- Do they have a ritual before or during what they do?
- Do they use visualisation skills?
- Have they got a lucky charm?
- How much training do they do?
- How many hours do they spend doing what they do?
- What makes them so good at what they do?

Take notes as you do the exercise. Once you are satisfied with your findings, model their confidence and ask for their feedback.

What can you do better next time? Were they able to see their strategy? And how did you feel?

Practise several times until you feel more at ease and comfortable. And find ways to make this new strategy your own, by adding your personality to it.

Isn't this a practical and fun way to Grow Confident?

I Want To Shape

As a child all I ever did was to dream,
I used to fantasise, I used to be.
I remember playing with my toys,
Constructing new cities and magical realities.
I modelled and I shaped,
I shaped and I modelled,
And I learned, I learned to do, I learned to be.
As a child I used to think everything was possible,
No dream was ever too big,
No fantasy ever too wild.
As a child all I ever did was to dream.
Now, I want to go back to those days.
I want to dream, I want to be.
I want to model, I want to shape.
Whatever it takes I will do,
I want to be, I want to do.
I want more of what it used to be
To learn and grow,
To grow and learn,
I dreamed, and I was
I let go of my dreams, I let go of myself.
Today I make a vow,
From now I will dream again, I will be again,
Let go of what held me back,
I will be me once more,
I am ready, I want it, I own it.

Step 6: Acting As If

"Acting is not about being someone different. It's finding the similarity in what is apparently different, then finding myself in there."

Meryl Streep

In this step I will be sharing with you what "acting as if" can do for your confidence, which ties in very closely with what we covered in the last step - modelling.

We all have heard the saying: "Fake it till you make it."

That is what acting as if is. Nothing else and nothing more.

I could easily leave it at that and let you explore this concept by yourself, but I won't.

Although everything I have shared with you so far I have found highly beneficial in my life, I would like you to look at this idea a bit more in detail.

Our mind on the whole is not able to tell the difference between a fact or truism and a fictional reality or truth.

By knowing and understanding this concept, we can now really start to understand how truly we are in charge of our reality, lives, the now and most importantly our future.

I write this chapter today, 1st of July, the current time is 30 minutes past midnight. By no means am I trying to show off and show you how committed I am - far from the truth. I am as guilty as the rest of procrastination and lack of discipline - that's just another story altogether.

The reason I have mentioned this is because earlier this evening I had a coaching call with a client. My coaching sessions are dynamic, interesting, educational, fun and experiential at times. So this client and I were talking about the future and what can be done to have a really good future.

Bear in mind this coaching session was done via Skype. I held a pen and paper to the camera and said: "This is all you need to know to create the future you want and desire. You have to take control of your decisions and ownership of your life. You ought to grab the pen and write your future."

I once heard this in an audio book - I believe it was 'Rich Dad, Poor Dad' by Robert Kiyosaki. He once attended a seminar in which a psychologist or someone similar said the difference between a pessimist and optimist is that the former sees a negative future whereas the latter sees a positive future. He then went on to say that the future isn't yet written. Either way is a lie, so why not make it a big, fat, juicy and ambitious lie, a lie of options and possibilities.

So, I am writing this for you to read, because this is what acting as if is. You start acting the way you want to be.

If your heart's desire is to be a musician, start acting like a musician. Do the things a musician would do, talk like a musician, eat like a musician, etc.

This is when we can start interweaving what we have learned so far.

That curiosity we mentioned in step 2 is what will give you the interest to want to know more and find out about whatever you want to create in the future. This then ties in with choosing to be better and healing the past, because you have learned what didn't work and what went wrong. And you also know how to model people's behaviours and skills.

When you are clear about what it is you want to accomplish and achieve in your life, remember exercise 3 in the chapter on modelling. You can further develop this exercise and, rather than modelling someone, you can act as if you were "that" and by "that" I mean the musician, teacher, mechanic, etc.

To bring it closer to the subject matter, you can start acting as if you were already confident.

How does a confident person stand?

How does a confident person breathe?

How does a confident person talk?

How does a confident person dress?

If you have already noticed that confident people do x, y or z, you can start acting like them. Do it right now!

Now that I start thinking about it, I would like to say that acting as if is the next step from modelling. It just makes sense to see how the "professionals," those who are really good at it, do it, so you then start acting as if you were like them too.

The next step from this is again repetition, the mother of all arts. The more you do it, the more comfortable you become, and so on. Just remember, your mind doesn't know whether you are "faking" or not. It is translated just the same.

You may be saying to yourself: "What would people say if they see me acting all weird and funny?"

I would then ask you: "Do they define who you are? Do they really care?

Are you going to give them control over you, your life and your future?"

To continue with my client's story, we have been clearing some limiting beliefs about the past. Surprise, surprise - there were some confidence "issues" there, but that is just irrelevant. We then moved on to the future, projecting the future the way he wants it to be, grabbing that pen and writing the future. He did all that and felt a relief about his future. He realised he had control over it - no one else does but himself.

We did some visualisation techniques about his near future and what it may hold for him. He was very specific about where he was and what he would be doing. There were a couple of pieces of information missing in that visualisation, though he got what he wanted from it.

So, toward the end of the coaching session, he screamed with joy and excitement and in ecstasy. I was so delighted I had that effect on him. However, his excitement stemmed from the fact that at that very second he received an email saying he had been given a grant for 6 months to pursue a research project anywhere in the world he wanted to. This grant is the enabling tool that will make that visualisation he did just earlier that evening a reality. Simply because he was just acting as if, his future had already happened and he was in control of it and in charge of his life.

Now he can truly say he is in control of his future and in charge of his life.

To be totally honest, I do not take any credit for his achievement and taking charge of his life. I was simply an enabler who allowed him to see his true potential, which had been there all along - he just didn't know it. Most importantly, it was his birthright all along.

When you act as if, what you are really saying is: "I know I haven't got it yet. I am working toward it and I will get it. It is just a matter of time!"

When you act as if you were a renowned author, what you are saying is: "I know I am not a renowned author yet. I am working on my book toward being a renowned author. I will be a renowned author. It is just a matter of time - work and believe!!!"

When you act as if you were confident, what you are saying is: "I know I am not confident yet. I am working toward being confident and I will be confident."

You do this, day in and day out, every day, every single day and guess what? You WILL be it - confident, a renowned author (just don't forget to write the book first!), etc.

Going back to what I shared with you in step 1, to what I called the darkest hour of my soul. When I emerged from it, yes I chose to be better and add value to the world and I was curious, and I was modelling and I was also doing my best to act as if I was OK. There was one thing I did act as if I had, and that was to smile. I faked smiling for many months. I acted as if I was naturally smiling. I had no reason to, yet I stuck to it, every day, day in and day out, every single day, smile, smile, smile. Until one day I actually started smiling naturally. I had finally cracked the smiling code, just because I acted as if I had reasons to smile.

For this to happen I repeated it, I repeated it, I repeated it until it became a habit. This habit then became part of me, my personality and my essence. Now I can't stop smiling. It just is one of my main features and people constantly comment on it and compliment me on it.

You may want to work on any area of your life that needs strengthening so you Grow Confident.

Just like modelling, acting as if is a good and very simple way of developing a new habit, which has the potential to then become part of your behaviour, which then becomes part of your personality.

Before I continue, I would like to give you the definition of what a habit is.

According to the Oxford Dictionary a habit is a settled or regular tendency or practice.

How simple is that?

A regular tendency or practice?

Even simpler, something you do time and time and time again, until it is so ingrained in you, that you just do it. You are so competent at it that you can even do it in your sleep.

I just had this thought, and to be honest, I should have written this before. However, being the way I am and believing in divine timing and intervention, I know this is the best and perfect time to mention it.

Why do you want to become or Grow Confident?

What is it that makes you believe you aren't confident or haven't any confidence?

Did you notice the difference in the two questions?

What makes you believe you aren't confident? This is a statement about your identity, you as the non-confident person.

On the other hand, what makes you believe you haven't any confidence? This is more of a capability - you do not have the skills or the knowledge (yet!) to be confident.

Which one of the two is it?

Are you lacking the skills to be confident?

Or, are you just not confident?

Also, I want to ask you what you want to accomplish by the end of this book. What will this new confidence give you? What will it enable you to do?

Keep these questions in mind as you continue your way through this book.

Let me explain to you why it is important to have a reason or motive to do anything in life and in general.

When you have an objective or focus, a target rather, you will give it your all. You will channel all of your energy, strength, thoughts, you name it, and you will give it all your might to accomplish it.

Nothing will stop you until you get to the finishing line.

Because when you value what you are getting, you will find the time, money and energy to make it happen. So how committed are you?

Acting As If: My Story

Before I tell you how I acted as if, I want to share with you why I decided to write this book.

Many of us have heard that we all have a book in us. Hence the amount of books in the book stores. We all want to share our story with the rest of the world.

In my case, I always had a passion for poetry and literature. I just loved it. I was fortunate enough to have great mentors and tutors, who taught me to love not only my language but writing in general.

So I thought I would become this incredible fiction author. My heart was set on writing a fiction book, which by the way I did write. I just didn't have the confidence to approach anyone about it and publish it. I put it to sleep and with it my desire to share it with the world.

The same with poetry. I had written hundreds and hundreds of poems throughout my life. Again, I felt inadequate and unworthy, and yes, you probably gathered it by now, I WAS NOT CONFIDENT TO APPROACH ANYONE ABOUT IT.

I lacked it, I wanted it, yet I failed to attain it. Confidence was so close, yet so far and out of reach.

I then started to act as if I had confidence. I had already done all I have shared with you so far:

- I chose to be better,
- I was curious,
- I healed the past,
- I learned from the past,
- I was modelling people,
- I was acting as if.

I was acting as if I had not just a bit, but tons of confidence. I thought: "You know what, if I am going to do this 'acting as if' thing, I will give it my all."

Oh boy, did I?

I will share with you two instances.

1. I was attending a networking event in London and I decided to arrive early. I love being on time and it also gives me control over the scene (one tip you may want to borrow from me, and allows you steer the conversations whichever way you want!

So there I was, walking like I owned not only the venue but the whole of London. I then started chatting and sharing with the attendees. I then came to a youngish man who said to me:

"I saw you come in earlier – I was outside, waiting for the right time to come in - and I have to say I felt blown away by you. The confidence you exuded was incredible. I thought to myself, I want to be like that."

I acknowledged what he said, smiled and I said: "I was pooping myself. I feel 100% nervous each and every time I attend a networking event."

He could not believe it, based on the way I presented myself.

This got me thinking. How much confidence or acting as if you had confidence do you need to blag it? To blend in? To feel comfortable? So that you are able to not only fit in but have the sense and feeling that you do belong, wherever you are or go or want to be?

2. This other example is with a friend of mine. Like many, every now and then I have a "let's get it all out" chat with friends so we free ourselves from unwanted and unnecessary thoughts.

On this occasion, he said he wished he had more confidence. (I thought: "Interesting, yet another person who wants a tiny bit more confidence.") He continued to share with me what attributes and qualities he thinks a confident person possesses. And even though he knows what a confident person looks like, most of his "closest" friends and acquaintances were not that.

Then I asked: "Who do you know, because you must at least know of one person who you can model and use as an example for confidence?"

I waited for his reply.

"You," he said.

Which, to be honest with you, I found both hard to believe and flattering at the same time, as this friend of mine has had senior roles for many years and knows a lot of "top" people, who I "expected" to have buckets, if not tons, of confidence.

He then proceeded to explain why he thought so and gave me some examples.

Again, I was humbled as to how people perceived me, and quite frankly I forgot how I got to be this confident.

I believe these two examples can demonstrate the power of acting as if. I started with a why, a reason to be more and Grow Confident. This was to give me self-belief and inner strength.

Since I have shown how important it is to define things in an almost universal manner, let's explore what the Oxford Dictionary says about confidence.

"Confidence, the belief that one can have faith in or rely on someone or something; a positive feeling arising from an appreciation of one's own abilities; self-assurance."

And "confident, 1 feeling confident in oneself. 2 feeling certainty about something."

Based on the definition above, it can be said that confidence and being confident starts with the self, so that you can then be confident or have confidence about something or someone else.

As already mentioned, I acted and acted and acted as if I had it. This practice of acting as if eventually became a habit, because my mind didn't know whether it was real or not.

That simple!

Now, I would like to share with you why I took the decision to write this book.

I have been interested in personal development since my teenage years. I wanted to understand more about life and people in general (curiosity), so personal development is not just very, but extremely, important to me. It was, it has been, it is and it will continue to be.

Though I did notice one thing and one thing only. No one ever talked about, or even considered touching on or working on, limiting beliefs, becoming better, growing as an individual and letting go of unwanted thoughts, beliefs and patterns.

Most of the books I have read give you the tools to work for what you want, like becoming a better communicator, getting better at drawing, becoming a better dancer, making your dreams come true.

Yet they fail at empowering people, because they have not got rid of unwanted beliefs and thoughts that hold them back.

As mentioned, I have read hundreds, if not thousands, of books, and I cannot think of one that says: "In order to get the life you want and benefit from the advice contained in this book, you have to work on your beliefs about yourself, your capabilities and/or confidence, so then you will be able to get the results you want because you have no objections or lack of drive."

I have known and heard of people who have spent a lot of money and have lost all of their faith and belief in personal development because they thought that by reading a book sort of "promising" you can have this (without doing much about the past) if you do that. And they have failed miserably time and time again.

My purpose is to do just the opposite. I want to work on the past (without dwelling on it!) so your present and future are better and brighter.

In my personal experience and based on my knowledge, you cannot move forward if you are being held back by a gigantic chain (in this case an imaginary one).

I want to help you to free yourself from those beliefs.

That's it. That simple.

I want you to take control of your life once again and do whatever you heart dictates to you.

Acting As If: Things To Avoid

There are many similarities between modelling and acting as if. Just like when you are modelling someone, you are not a "fraud" or a "fake" when you act as if.

On the contrary, what you are doing is borrowing a belief about what is possible, of who you can become and what you can do.

Just because you didn't have something or didn't know how to develop it, it doesn't mean that you weren't born to have it too.

The number one dream killer isn't the dream stealers (those are people who mock our dreams and fantasies when we share them with them), but us ourselves, because we never develop ourselves to a level that matches what we want.

I have said it before, and here it goes again. To get what you want, you have to step out of the "victim" mentality and start adopting the owner, master, ruler, developer and creator of your own life. To simplify it even further, you can be the builder of your wishes and wants in life.

How powerful is it to say to people: "I have created all I have. It took me some doing and effort, but it was worth it. Now I have it all!"?

Acting As If: The Exercises

1. Affirmations

If, like me, you have been working on your personal and professional development for a while, you must have heard of using affirmations.

To help you clarify this concept, I will define the verb to affirm. To affirm is to make a formal declaration rather than taking an oath.

So, an affirmation is when we declare to ourselves that we are committed, serious, and, most importantly, will do whatever it takes to ensure we accomplish that which we are affirming.

I will repeat it again (or copy and paste it if you prefer!).

An affirmation is when we declare to ourselves that we are committed, serious, and, most importantly, will do whatever it takes to ensure we accomplish that which we are affirming.

How powerful is that?

Who is control?

YOU are…

I will be honest with you - I was not the type of person who was into affirmations. Then suddenly (when I was prepared for it) I noticed how simple and empowering it was, to train your mind, develop a new belief system, overcome old unnecessary paradigms and programme new ideas and concepts in your head. And we also create new neurological pathways, as our brain is working in a new way.

How do you create a powerful affirmation?

There is no right or wrong way to do an affirmation. However, there are some guidelines:

- It is best if it is written in the present tense and in a positive manner, using the formula: I am…
- Example: I am a confident man. Wherever I go, I feel I can do and accomplish whatever I put my mind do. The sky is the limit.
- It has got to be personal to you, have some energy and feeling to it.
- It helps to say an affirmation out loud and visualise it as you do so.

If it helps, I want you to imagine an affirmation as a goal you want to accomplish. So when you say that affirmation out loud, you are saying and affirming to yourself and the world: "This is what I want. Hear me and pay attention to my words, because I never ever compromise my integrity or the integrity of my words."

Isn't this so strong and powerful to get you moving and Growing Confident?

Here is what I want you to do.

Write down a list of 30 affirmations, which you will commit to affirm and say out loud daily - in the morning, at lunchtime and before bed.

If you are serious about this "Growing Confident" business, you will do it. And I guarantee you will notice the difference in the way you see yourself and any challenges that may arise from then on.

These affirmations can be about anything. Use your curiosity and imagination, be as creative as you possibly can.

Use the space provided or use your journal.

Two wonderful things happen here. As I said, think of an affirmation as a goal. Statistically, goals that are written down are more likely to be achieved. And when you say or affirm these affirmations out loud, you are essentially making yourself accountable for this happening, which is a great way of ensuring you get it done.

Note. When you want to really ensure you accomplish your goals, tell someone what you are planning to do, and ask them to ask you about your progress and probe if it hasn't been done and why!

My Affirmations:

1. ______________________________
2. ______________________________
3. ______________________________
4. ______________________________
5. ______________________________
6. ______________________________
7. ______________________________
8. ______________________________
9. ______________________________
10. ______________________________
11. ______________________________
12. ______________________________
13. ______________________________
14. ______________________________
15. ______________________________
16. ______________________________
17. ______________________________
18. ______________________________
19. ______________________________
20. ______________________________
21. ______________________________
22. ______________________________
23. ______________________________
24. ______________________________
25. ______________________________
26. ______________________________
27. ______________________________
28. ______________________________
29. ______________________________
30. ______________________________

2. What Do I Want To Improve?

1. ____________________
2. ____________________
3. ____________________
4. ____________________
5. ____________________
6. ____________________
7. ____________________
8. ____________________
9. ____________________
10. ____________________
11. ____________________
12. ____________________
13. ____________________
14. ____________________
15. ____________________
16. ____________________
17. ____________________
18. ____________________
19. ____________________
20. ____________________
21. ____________________
22. ____________________
23. ____________________
24. ____________________
25. ____________________
26. ____________________
27. ____________________
28. ____________________
29. ____________________
30. ____________________

Now, rewrite the improvements as affirmations.

1. ____________________
2. ____________________
3. ____________________
4. ____________________
5. ____________________
6. ____________________
7. ____________________
8. ____________________
9. ____________________
10. ____________________
11. ____________________
12. ____________________
13. ____________________
14. ____________________
15. ____________________
16. ____________________
17. ____________________
18. ____________________
19. ____________________
20. ____________________
21. ____________________
22. ____________________
23. ____________________
24. ____________________
25. ____________________
26. ____________________
27. ____________________
28. ____________________
29. ____________________
30. ____________________

3. What I Want To Accomplish, Do & Have

1. ___
2. ___
3. ___
4. ___
5. ___
6. ___
7. ___
8. ___
9. ___
10. ___
11. ___
12. ___
13. ___
14. ___
15. ___
16. ___
17. ___
18. ___
19. ___
20. ___
21. ___
22. ___
23. ___
24. ___
25. ___
26. ___
27. ___
28. ___
29. ___
30. ___

Rewrite the list as affirmations now:

1. ______________________________
2. ______________________________
3. ______________________________
4. ______________________________
5. ______________________________
6. ______________________________
7. ______________________________
8. ______________________________
9. ______________________________
10. ______________________________
11. ______________________________
12. ______________________________
13. ______________________________
14. ______________________________
15. ______________________________
16. ______________________________
17. ______________________________
18. ______________________________
19. ______________________________
20. ______________________________
21. ______________________________
22. ______________________________
23. ______________________________
24. ______________________________
25. ______________________________
26. ______________________________
27. ______________________________
28. ______________________________
29. ______________________________
30. ______________________________

4. Create A Vision Board

A vision board is a powerful visual reminder of our goals and wants in life.

Whatever you want to manifest, attract and create in your life, pin it on your vision board.

Hang it in a place so you can see it at all times and remind yourself of what it is you want.

To create one, which needn't be expensive, use cut-outs from magazines or newspapers and either glue or pin them on a message board or cardboard.

A few guidelines to create the perfect vision board:

- Include all areas of your life - finances, family, health, social etc.
- Keep it private. Only you should be able to see it – it's private and personal.
- Look at it daily - in the morning, during the day and at night before you go to bed.
- Give those goals a deadline.
- Visualise those images as if they had already happened in your life. What do they feel like? What do you see? What do you hear?
- Have a strategy in place to make it happen.

This is where some people go wrong. They think that by having a vision board, reading a book and doing some affirmations the world will stop at their feet and give it to them.

Well, I AM SORRY, you've got to work for it! Work for it! Make it happen! Put some energy behind it! Show the world and the universe you want it and you want it bad.

See what works and what doesn't work to make your dreams come true. Put your strategies into place and adjust them as needed, until you get what you want.

Isn't this a great way to get, become and Grow Confident?

5. Keep Journaling!

I mentioned that one of my journals is the wants/dreams journal. See what you have written there so far, and make those into affirmations too.

Keep track of your thoughts and actions.

Have fun too!!!

Personal growth and development needn't be painful - it can be fun too.

Choose A Way

In life I learned to pretend and hide,
I knew nothing else, nothing else mattered.
Day in and day out,
Day out and day in.
I felt there was something missing,
What could I do to make it all better?
Move elsewhere and start afresh?
I have learned to not be.
Wouldn't it be incredible to pretend so I could be?
Find a way in which I can act,
Do it often and enough so I then became.
Wouldn't it be great to do this?
So my life I controlled too,
Choose a way to simply be,
Act, not pretend,
And by acting becoming and growing,
Wouldn't this be nice
if I simply could?

Step 7: Being Open

"The hardest thing about being a leader is demonstrating or showing vulnerability. When the leader demonstrates vulnerability and sensibility and brings people together, the team wins."

Howard Schultz

This step will give you food for thought as to why it is OK to be open and be in touch with your emotions.

In every person's story there is a phase in their lives of either resistance or nothingness, in which we find ourselves in limbo, not knowing what our next steps will be, nor what the final destination will be.

I too had a moment of resistance. For me this resistance was being open.

If we go back to what I have said so far, you will recall I have said a number of times how conditioned we are. Sometimes people do it unintentionally and for others it is intentional.

For me, this conditioning was being in touch with my emotions and being open.

As a good Latin boy from a very early age I was told: "Little boys don't cry, boys don't cry, young men don't cry, men don't cry, real men don't cry."

Needless to ask why our patriarchal, macho-dominated society is the way it is.

I am sorry if the above statement offends anyone or triggers a resistance or whatever it may bring forth.

I had years and years of emotional baggage adhered to me like the "plague." I was not the most empathetic person nor patient. Even for a gay guy I would make macho comments about other gays, or even women. I would never cry in public and I would show how macho I was because I could, and that's what I was brought up to believe.

Did it serve me in any possible way?

Obviously NOT!

When I take my lessons from the past, I can say very sincerely: "Yes, it helped me to fight my corner and for my causes." (By fight, I do not mean physically - I am against fighting!) It allowed me to protect my nearest and dearest from others. It helped me with developing my confidence.

At the same time it took its toll on how I expressed myself, how I communicated to others and the world.

I had very little control, or no control whatsoever, over my emotions. I was not going to give in and show emotions in public or to anyone for that matter.

I had a strategy that I learned from my stepfather. Once or twice a year, in the first and second half of the year, I would cry.

Whether there was a reason or not for it, I would do it anyway. At times there was alcohol involved, which would help me get rid of those "things" called tears.

Did it serve me in any possible way?

You could say so. Yet at the same time it didn't, because I did not know if what I was experiencing was an accumulation of things, or just a tear so I could feel better about myself, being able to show emotions.

When I started my different trainings, at first it was very difficult to watch people cry in public. ("Boys and people shouldn't cry in public," I would hear the voice saying in my head!) I felt sick to my stomach. I could not understand why and what effects it could have in their lives.

Even though I am openly gay, on more than one occasion I would be put under the spotlight because of my apparent dissociation from the events and my emotions, which was "unusual."

For years I found myself questioning this "lack of" or inability to express my emotions like a "normal" person, or be open like animals and children and older people.

So, I embarked on this quest to find my open side, my openness.

I felt I was the missing character from "The Wizard of Oz" - the human seeking his openness…

Sadly, there was no mystical wizard in my "Yellow Brick Road" and my "Emerald City." I was alone with my lack of emotions and openness.

As I have mentioned umpteen times by now, I have always been very curious, so this question was in the back of my head constantly: "Why am I not as open as the rest of the world?"

I was observing people, doing my best to learn from their ability (that's how I saw it) to show their open side and model it, so I could then act as if I was open too! I promise you, I tried and tried and tried to be like them and I couldn't.

By now, you have probably gathered that I was trying, not really doing it or being.

One evening in my house, I was sitting on my sofa, talking to a friend of mine. She is in marketing and sales, so we were talking about ways for me to promote myself and my services.

When our "business" chat ended, she said to me: "I recently read a really interesting article about successful people and openness. The fact that they are in touch with their emotions and are open makes them better at what they do and successful as a direct result!"

My ears stood higher than they had ever done. I had found the answer to my question, the solution to my riddle.

Openness = success, success = mastery. So to be successful, I had to master my emotions.

Easy, isn't it?

At least it sounds it.

In practice it probably was a whole lot more complex than that.

Hearing those words from my friend was a paradigm shift on its own. If I wanted to be successful at what I did, all I had to do was master my emotions. The rest would follow - not only success but confidence, better relationships, enhanced communication, better listening. I can go on and on and on, because that is how powerful it is.

When you are open, you can say:

"I messed up. I am human and I am owning the consequences, whatever they may be."

Or:

"I am going through a rough time in my life. I want some help, because I know it will help me get to where I want to be in life."

Or:

"I am emotionally closed and I know it doesn't serve me in any way. I want to be able to feel, just the same as everybody else."

Do you not find these statements powerful in their own right?

I cannot remember whether I have said this before or not, so here it goes:

"My idea of real personal development, growth or evolution is not doing things right - it is doing what is right. It isn't about successes or achieving wealth. Personal development isn't about becoming better than others. Personal development is about four key things:

- Self-discipline,
- Evolution and growth,
- Mastery and
- Ownership.

The last one is perhaps the one I refer to the most - OWNERSHIP. You own your words, you own your actions, you own your results and, most importantly, you own yourself, YOUR LIFE."

I fully got it and understood it when I mastered my emotions.

It was not easy for me. For you it may be totally different. You may have no difficulty with it.

Once I came out of this "vacuum" and lack of emotions, I soared like the Phoenix from the ashes of yesteryears, of conquered limiting beliefs, of overcome fears. I came out truly triumphant and I was emotionally sane, because I knew I was in control of my emotions, not them of me.

Going back to ownership, I tell myself (as I always start with myself, before I share with anyone), my friends, my family and my clients: "To get what you want in life, you have to own your decisions. You must own your thoughts and your every action, or else they will take over and control you instead."

True mastery is saying to oneself: "I am in charge or my life and I control what I do or don't do." Isn't this a real sign of confidence?

Being open has allowed me to honour all those 6 steps we have mentioned already. I chose to better and I owned that decision. I was curious and I owned that curiosity. I healed my past and I owned that process. I learned from the past and I owned that learning. I modelled great models and I owned that choice. I acted as if and I owned that behaviour so I could get to where I am right now.

Because I mastered how I felt about myself, others and life, I wake up every day and say to myself, looking at myself in the eyes: "I love you." Because it's OK to feel emotions as long as you are in control.

Don't you want a bit of this too?

Imagine yourself in a future situation where openness and the mastery of your emotions is required. How empowered will you feel afterwards?

Being Open: My Story

Even though I have probably told you a great deal of how I was able to be and become open, I will source some more tales to share with you, so you can see the real importance of mastering your emotions.

As a trainer of EFT (Emotional Freedom Techniques) and NLP (Neuro-Linguistic Programming), it is somewhat expected of you to know it all.

There was a particular occasion when I was talking about the NLP communication model, which is key and essential to know when you are learning NLP. On this particular occasion I was asked a question about the brain and how it related to what I was explaining.

I looked at the student, smiled and acknowledged his question, and I said: "I do not know." It felt so good, so freeing and empowering to say: "No, I do not know," rather than blag it and then being exposed for it.

Thankfully, one of the students was a psychologist and she was able to explain in a scientific yet coherent manner what he wanted to know.

Also, I was delighted to welcome her to the front and explain to everyone what she knew.

If I had been "emotionally" incoherent, I would have messed it up badly. So, my integrity and professionalism would have been compromised, had I not admitted I didn't know.

Mastery is much more than knowing how to control or compose yourself. It is also about honesty, it is about being realistic, it is about being OK with yourself. It is about not attaching yourself to any outcome, be it positive or not.

This reminds me of one of the biggest and single most valuable pieces of information, which comes from my mentor's lifetime research, Silvia Hartmann.

The Aspects Model

I will do my very best to keep the purity of what Silvia talks about in The Aspects Model.

"One single person can only inhabit one single state AT A TIME, thus creating a sequential incongruence between different aspects of the same person across time.

We have – infinite - aspects, not because a person's time of life is infinite, but because you can make infinitely smaller distinctions from one aspect to the next – one second, a tenth of a second, a billionth of a second, a google of a second, and so on - infinitely.

In the Aspects Model, "I" exists always and only in the here and now.

A person is here in the now; and the memory (or data) is about what happened to an aspect then."

Here is an illustration of The Aspect Model.

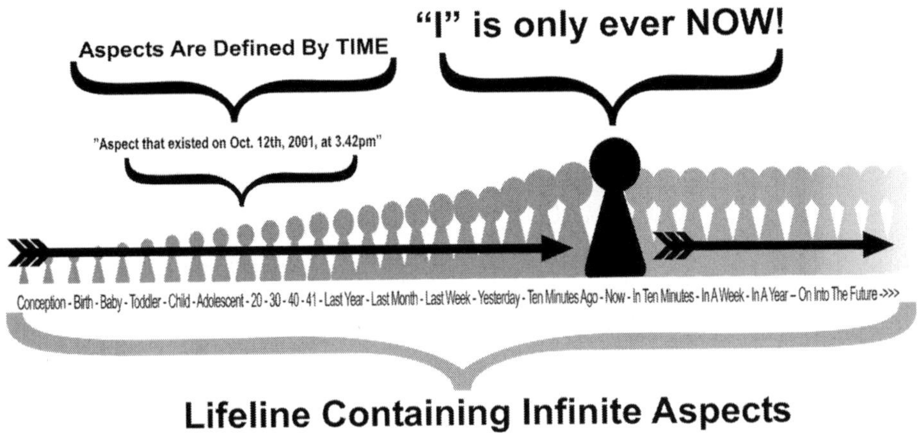

With thanks to Silvia Hartmann, EFT Master Practitioner Manual, 2011.

When I saw this diagram and fully understood it, I realised what a life-changing model this is. By naming our former and even future selves "aspects," we can get out of our own way, not attach to any outcome and get lessons from the past without getting upset about it.

The best thing is that it solves the problem how you can really love yourself. Or heal "yourself." You love your aspects, you heal your aspects. That is the strong you in the now, and you can reach out to past and future aspects too and give them your love and support. It's easy when you know how!

Isn't this model just worth your money? I strongly encourage you to find out more about it or contact someone who may help you understand it.

This model helped me to really master my emotions and remain neutral about it, getting to the root of some of my "issues" and obtaining a wealth of information which helped me to get to where I am.

Another example I can give you of how I became open and really put what I learned into practice was on one occasion on the phone to my mother.

I love my mother very much. Though, being my mother, she knows how to trigger me and what buttons to push to get a reaction. (Sorry mother!)

For years many of our conversations could have been scripted. We spent the same amount of time on the phone, same questions, same answers, same complaints (on her behalf), etc. etc. etc.

Before I fully tell you what happened, in the past when my mother triggered something in me (or that aspect of mine, to use Silvia's language and model here), I would go ballistic and argue back to a point where our voices would be raised, things would be said, then more things would be said. The past would be brought up (by us both!), there would be an exchange of inappropriate language and either one of us would end up hanging the phone up.

This may sound familiar to some of you, it may not.

This particular day, we started following our script (they do come in handy sometimes). We were very civil at the beginning, most of the conversation was positive and uplifting, then suddenly my mother made a comment, which some people would consider catty, patronising and even putting me down.

I continued listening to her for a few seconds. I could feel my heart racing so fast, the bomb was ticking, and before it was too late I said: "Mother, I do respect and appreciate your opinion. However, I have taken your comment personally. Could you please stop it or I will end the call?"

I could hear in my mother's voice the surprise, horror and even shock. She just decided to continue her negative comments.

Then I said in a very calm, cool and collected manner: "Mother, I said I would hang up if you didn't stop and you continued to undermine me with your comments. Please do not take this personally, for it isn't my intention, but I do not wish to hear such words and comments that do no good to either of us. So goodbye for now and I will speak to you real soon."

For the first time in my entire life and in the history of my relationship with my mother, I felt I was in control of the situation. Please do not misinterpret my words - I am saying in control of the situation, by no means do I mean of my mother or her life.

I chose to not let my emotions get in the way by saying: "Hey Mon, that is not cool, I do not like it -" (As a way of warning her) "- please stop or else I will end the call." That simple!

There is nothing wrong with handling an inappropriate conversation like this. You say it as it is, in a polite manner and see it through if necessary.

Being able to do this showed me I was mastering my emotions, and also demonstrated to my mother how courageous and confident I was to say: "No, mother - enough!"

Mastery needn't be about arrogance or being conceited. It is about honesty and openness.

When you are open, you are free, light and you just are!

Do it and you will see what I mean.

Being Open: Things to avoid

Although there isn't anything to be concerned about when you are open, I would highlight a few things that I would personally avoid:

- Be careful in front of whom you are open. There are times when some people can take advantage of situations and/or people.
- Being open does not mean manipulating others. I urge you to speak from the heart when you are open, or you could find yourself in an "awkward" position.
- When you are open, do not bring the past into the current situation. This may open unhealed wounds and cause you a lot more grief than you bargain for.
- When you are open, get the positive lesson from it, take it with you and move on. Do not dwell on it; you want to master your emotions not to worsen them.
- Being open does not mean you are exposed. On the contrary, it says: "I am well protected and nothing can harm me."
- Remember, when you are open you do not lose control. On the contrary, you have the reins over that openness - use it wisely.

Being Open: The Exercises

I know and I firmly believe you have been doing all your exercises in this book so far. If not, stop right now and get started.

I do not wish to hear excuses. If you are committed to your personal growth and Growing Confident, you will do them, and I will hold you accountable for completing them.

Nothing would fill my heart more than receiving an email with these exercises done, at least one, and saying how it has positively impacted your life.

Make a list of how you would like to be more open

You, more than anybody else, know what areas of your life you need to soften and become more open with. Do an honest list to help you be a master of these emotions.

As before, write your statements down, put them to one side and a day or so later, read them again.

Review them and add or take some away until you are satisfied.

1. I Want To Be More Open About/With ...

1. ____________________
2. ____________________
3. ____________________
4. ____________________
5. ____________________
6. ____________________
7. ____________________
8. ____________________
9. ____________________
10. ____________________
11. ____________________
12. ____________________
13. ____________________
14. ____________________
15. ____________________
16. ____________________
17. ____________________
18. ____________________
19. ____________________
20. ____________________
21. ____________________
22. ____________________
23. ____________________
24. ____________________
25. ____________________
26. ____________________
27. ____________________
28. ____________________
29. ____________________
30. ____________________

Now you have your list. What can you do next?

I invite you to think of ways in which you can become more open in whichever area you chose.

Let me give you an example. If in the previous exercise I wrote down:

- I want to me more open when telling someone I love them.

Now, I need a strategy or a way in which I could do this.

I could start by telling people I love them, and see how I react when they say it back.

How do I feel?

Does it remind me of a past event?

Do I need more practice before I attempt this?

Do this with all of them, so you have a strategy in place.

Though, when it comes to carrying it out, focus on one at a time only.

Just as I have advised you before, write any insights, thoughts or ideas in your journal.

2. What Strategy Will I Use To Be More Open?

1. ________________
2. ________________
3. ________________
4. ________________
5. ________________
6. ________________
7. ________________
8. ________________
9. ________________
10. ________________
11. ________________
12. ________________
13. ________________
14. ________________
15. ________________
16. ________________
17. ________________
18. ________________
19. ________________
20. ________________
21. ________________
22. ________________
23. ________________
24. ________________
25. ________________
26. ________________
27. ________________
28. ________________
29. ________________
30. ________________

3. The Unconventional Exercise

I highly recommend you watch a romantic film and/or chick flick!

Yes, you are reading right!!!

These kind of movies connect with us at an emotional level. If you are embarking on a journey where you want to explore and master your emotions, then a good movie will do that.

I will give you a list of my favourite films. They get me every time.

So, here they are - in no particular order.

- Precious, 2009.
- Legally Blonde, 2001.
- The Magic Bubble, 1992.
- The Lake House, 2006.
- Love and Other Drugs, 2010.
- Bridesmaids, 2011.
- Enemy Mine, 1985.
- Titanic, 1997.
- Broke back Mountain, 2005.
- Practical Magic, 1998.

Watch these movies and let the emotions flow. If I can urge you to watch two of these films, please ensure you watch Precious and The Magic Bubble.

4. Read a Romantic Story

Yes, you are reading right, again!

I have found that some of the most profound emotional breakthroughs I have had have been through reading a good book.

When you read a good book, you just are - everything else ceases to exist. It is just the book and you, nothing else.

If you have watched The Never Ending Story you will know what I mean. You feel as if you were part of the book.

I will leave this exercise up to you.

Though I will share with you some of my favourites.

- Veronica Decides to Die - Paulo Coelho,
- By the River Piedra I Sat Down and Wept - Paulo Coelho,
- Great Expectations - Charles Dickens,
- 100 Years of Solitude - Gabriel Garcia Marquez.

You may have read a book that has touched your life in the past. Read it again, and again and again, so you feel the emotions coming to the surface.

5. Listen to Romantic Music

We all have our classic favourites, do not deny it… (I do!)

ABBA? Whitney Houston? Leona Lewis?

I have put this as an exercise, for the same reason as before. There are times when the lyrics and the rhythm of the music touch our soul and emotions. And we feel this warmth and these emotions, which are there for us to access and embrace.

I can mention some of my favourite artists - you may have your own. As long as you listen to some romantic music, I don't mind who you listen to.

Here is a list of some of my favourite artists:

- Celine Dion,
- Lara Fabian,
- Whitney Houston,
- Mariah Carey,
- Christina Aguilera,
- Shania Twain.

If it helps you, here is a list of some of my favourite songs:

- I Turn to You - Christina Aguilera,
- The Power of the Dream - Celine Dion,
- Broken Vow - Lara Fabian,
- The Winner Takes It All - ABBA,
- I Have Nothing - Whitney Houston,
- Hero - Mariah Carey.

Listen to the songs, time and time again, and let the emotions come to the surface. Remember, you have nothing to fear, you are in control.

True mastery requires practice. Get practising right now.

Living Open

No more lies, no more suffering,
I have hidden myself in the cells of my body,
I want to be, I choose to be.
I lived many lives of lie and deceit,
Please set me free,
Life isn't what I planned it to be.
I got lost, yet the roads never led to any salvation,
I cried and I begged,
Take my life away, set me free.
In vain I travelled over valleys of sorrow,
I choose to be, I want to be,
What must I do to finally be?
Please, show me some mercy,
I am ready to embrace my destiny,
Take control of my life and honour it.
This is who I am, this is all I am,
Take me or leave me, the choice is yours,
I have lived, I have learned.
I fear not, for I have chosen to be,
And by being I bear it all,
I do not care, I do not mind.
This is who I am, this is all I am,
I am human, I am me,
Open, happy but free.

Step 8: Telling Your Story To The World

"Every story I create, creates me. I write to create myself."

Octavo E. Butler

In this step, like me, I will share with you the importance of telling your story to the world, why your story matters and how it can positively impact the life of someone you know or the life of someone you don't know yet.

There are many reasons why telling our story is important, though for me the biggest reason is that, by sharing with others what we have gone through, done and learned, these people have the ability, or option rather, to also learn from it, if they wish.

As you have read time and time again - I am very curious. This curiosity got me interested in people's stories and their biographies, their success stories, their failures and obstacles, how they overcame them and what came next.

Another element or advantage of telling our story, or in fact any story, is that we are all storytellers. Telling a story is such a compelling way to convey a message, especially when our brains speak and translate everything into metaphors, so the data or memories can be retrieved much more easily in the future by using analogies, comparison and contrasting.

If there hadn't been stories to be told and storytellers to tell these stories, the world wouldn't be as we know it. There would be no teaching and learning, we would not have the technology advancement we have at present, nor would we be as coherent and sound as we are as a race.

When we switch the TV or radio on, we all hear stories. These stories, however, are stories of despair, disaster, pain, hurt, hatred, anger, corruption, injustice. And I could write a very extensive list, so you get the idea.

Would it not be more powerful to wake up to stories of empowerment, success, love, happiness, joy, hope? Do not get me wrong or misinterpret what I am saying here. We do hear these sorts of stories in the media - not enough though. I would say the ratio of negative to positive stories is 10:1, if not higher.

With the social media boom (which I can say with conviction we all are part of), now more than ever before we see the truth and reality of what is happening around us almost instantaneously. Can you see the impact this has in people's lives?

Let me ask you a question and please answer honestly.

When you post, write or share on social media, what message are you giving to those in your networks, or the world if you may?

Are you sending a message of negativity and despair?

Examples:

My life is a mess. I can't believe I have done it again. Will I ever learn?

Oh God, I am so stupid. I got drunk and made a fool of myself.

I hate my life.

My partner is an idiot, he cheated on me. Why is he doing this to me?

The examples above I have read, seen over and over again on social media.

What do you think your friends on Facebook, Twitter, Google+, YouTube, etc. can see of your life?

Have you noticed any patterns or trends since you started actively using social media?

I can talk from observation and personal experience. I have noticed a decrease in the numbers of friends I have, who are not posting anything negative.

Social media have transformed our lives in a very incredible and useful way, though it reminds me of the proverbial "double-edged" sword. You must know how to use it, otherwise it can have some severe consequences.

Needless to say, whatever we say or post on social media will be there for evermore and has the potential to come back to us and hurt us in years to come. It has already happened to some.

On the other hand, are you the kind of person who is writing, posting messages of hope, love, life, friendship, solidarity, empowerment and positivity?

Examples:

I am very blessed and privileged to have some wonderful and supportive friends and family. They lift me up.

My children fill my life with joy. They are my light and heart, they bring so much happiness to our lives.

I have recently volunteered to help the less fortunate children and I have learned how important it is to give more to those in need.

When you check your feeds on social media (and this is me making the total assumption that you too are on social media), what message do you notice the most?

"What has this got to do with Growing Confident?" I may hear you screaming at this book.

Everything, absolutely everything.

Stop reading this book, and I encourage you to take a look at your feeds on Facebook for instance.

You will probably notice someone posting photos of their night out, with some distasteful images and wording. You will see violence, you will notice anger, hatred, you will read people's negativity.

If you are lucky, you may even notice 1 or 2 positive messages - that is, if they are not being buried by the negative messages.

When what you say impacts positively in the lives of others, you naturally grow as an individual, because people start telling you and making comments about what you are sharing, as well as saying it to others.

This then translates into belief in yourself, which then becomes confidence. Again, because you know that what you are saying and doing is for the highest good of those around you - family, friends, acquaintances, etc.

To tell your story you needn't go to the extreme of writing a book. You can start taking some baby, tiny steps. You can start by expressing yourself more positively, watch what you post on social media, pay attention to what you say and how you say it. At this point I would like to make you aware of three things:

1. We are rubbish communicators. No-one teaches us how to effectively communicate, nor to listen more and think before we say things. Let me reassure you, I have been guilty of this many times, and I still do it!
2. During the communication process there are three things we must remember at all times: 7% is our words (language used), 38% how we say it (intonation) and 55% is our body language or non-verbal language. You do not know how your "story" is impacting the life of others. When you post, for instance, people cannot hear your voice nor can they watch your body language. There is a void of 93% where a lot can go wrong. Pay great attention to what you say, how you say it and what your body is saying.
3. Any communication has four parts: the sender (the person who talks), the receiver (the person listening), the message (what is being said) and the feedback (the way the information/message has been understood). I will not go into great details about all of these. Just look into it and improving your communication skills. In NLP there are a set of presuppositions, things that you take as true. Two of these presuppositions say: "The meaning of communication is the response you get." How powerful is this? What sort of response are you getting? The other one says: "You cannot not communicate." (Yes, a double-negative.) It is so clear and true. It doesn't matter what you do or say, you always communicate!

Another way you can tell your story to the world is by blogging. This is a fun and cheap way of sharing our wants and message with the world. You can also write poetry or, even simpler than this, treat people the way you would like to be treated. This is a bold and empowering message. You say to people: "I am nice to you, you are nice to me and together we change the world."

So far we have chosen to be better and awakened our curiosity. We have healed or are in the process of healing our past, we have learned and are still learning from the past (this is an ongoing process). We have been modelling excellence, skills and techniques, we have started acting as if we were x, y, z (and you will be it, as long as you repeat it often enough), we have accepted to be open and that openness is a good thing. And now we are telling our story to the world, while Growing Confident and adding value to other people's lives.

How much more than this do you want? By you becoming and being better, you empower and inspire others to follow your example and lead.

Confidence is much more than being "comfortable" in your own shoes and with your actions. By serving as a role model to others and bringing back that message of hope, love and happiness, you show people that in order to do and to have, firstly and foremost they must be.

Telling Your Story To The World: My Story

I believe it may be apparent by now that this book is partly my story. I am sharing with you what I did to Grow Confident. I am telling the world that there is hope. There is much more out there as long as we get out of our own way and our heads and go for it.

So, I feel now is the time to tell you a bit more about me, my real story, the person behind these words.

I was born in 1983, 19th of July in Panama City, Panama. I wish I could tell you what the first 4-5 years of my life were like. They just seem to have vanished and left no evidence of what was before I started remembering more about my former years.

There are just flashes of memories which I cannot make much sense of. At this point I would like to mention an important fact I recently learned, that between the ages of 0-6 we are in a hypnotic state, in a trance essentially, which would explain why many of us remember very little about our former years.

It is in these years that most of our limiting beliefs and absurd decisions are made and we carry them with us (like that rucksack mentioned earlier!) throughout our lives…

This having been said, I have recollection of my life from the age of 5½ onwards. My mother and my stepfather (whom I grew up believing was my real father) and I lived in a small flat in the suburbs of Panama City. It wasn't the most affluent of places, nor the poorest, yet you could see some people were struggling to make ends meet.

I have no idea how long we were there for. It all seemed a short period of time. However, my parents put all their life savings in to buy their own house, which was marginally bigger than the flat we had. The only difference was, this was ours and we had a garden and some room for expansion, if had we the money for it.

In the summer of 1989 (bear in mind, our summer is December to May) I started my first year in primary school. I was so excited, I felt like a real "grown up." The school I attended was by my grandmother's house for convenience purposes.

Needless to say, I remember very little about this big phase of my life due to the fact that is was overshadowed by the invasion of Panama by the Americans in order to catch Colonel Manuel Antonio Noriega. I did not know what was happening. I was a child who just wanted to play and explore, learn and be curious.

Because of the invasion, we only did two terms out of four and we decided to spend some time in the countryside where my mother was from. If my memory doesn't fail me, we must have spent four months or so there, waiting for the situation in the capital city to improve and go back to normal.

1990 came, and I started a new school. I was getting to know my new neighbours and I was given a bicycle. I loved it, though it was a challenge at first and I got the scratches at the time to prove it.

One of the highlights of having moved to where we did in Cerro Batea was the fact we were 3 doors away from my auntie and cousins. Although I used to see them as my siblings, for some strange reason things changed and we didn't play as much as we used to. The relationship was not close any more.

I was not particularly enjoying school. I felt I was out of place. In 1991, things were different. I didn't know my mother was pregnant. In fact, I just thought she got really fat. In November of that year, this little boy appears. I was confused. It was explained to me that he was my little brother and I was encouraged to look after him.

I will never forget his birthday, nor him. For that day, the day he was born, 7th of November 1991, while my mother was in labour, I was being looked after by my cousin. While he was distracted watching TV, I was playing with a plastic bag and a lighter. You can imagine what comes next. The plastic bag starts to melt and I am desperately doing my best to make it stop so I don't ruin anything. In the end it landed just above my right knee - it was painful, I must add!

The years that came after that were almost the same. During the summer holidays we would go nowhere, we would do next to nothing. The only thing I had to look forward to was Christmas and going back to school, so I could have some sanity back in my life - and even that wasn't enough for me.

I am not going to deny the dynamics in our household changed. My mother devoted her life to my brother. At that time I didn't understand why, now I do. My brother was the child from the love of her life and I wasn't. She saw him in her son and I was a reminder of other memories she perhaps wished she'd forgotten.

By now I believe you can see my life didn't differ much from many people. In fact, it probably makes you realise how fortunate you are to have had the one you did.

During my puberty I did not know what was happening to me. It was all weird and new and scary. I noticed my body started to change. I was growing taller and my physique was changing too. My voice deepened and suddenly I became a young man.

By this time I knew I was different, and by different I mean gay. I had the "name calling" at school, in the neighbourhood, even some family members would make remarks about my sexuality.

Having been born in a Catholic country I knew just too well what a sin was, and we were reminded every Sunday at church, so I was all too clear that my preference or orientation was sinful, shameful and worthy of punishment, at least by their standards.

It was during this time that I was ashamed of myself and I created this façade, pretending I was someone I wasn't, pretending I was confident when deep down I wasn't. In this phase of my life I didn't know what acting as if was, I just pretended.

Though I was "confident" on the outside, I knew what was going on inside. I knew just too well that I was different and all I wanted was to be "normal" and fit in, be able to marry, have children and lead a "normal" life like people around me. I didn't need a reminder of what people saw me as, so I would write on the back of my notebooks, and it would always be the same: "God, why me? Why me, God?"

Time and time and time again, I would write it in all of my notebooks, all of them and it wouldn't be just one page, but many.

God, why me? Why me, God?

God, why me? Why me, God?

God, why me? Why me, God?

On one occasion, one of my peers sat on my chair and opened the notebook that was on the desk and she read and proceeded to make fun of me.

I felt like dying. My mask had been taken off, I was exposed and almost ridiculed. I felt powerless.

She didn't tell anyone nor did she know what that meant. I just felt like that.

My act continued through the next 5 years. I had not been out of Panama City for about 10 or so years, so my life was all I knew, and I did not like it.

In 1999 things changed, or were meant to change. I made the decision to do my Holy Communion and confirmation. I thought that the only way I could make peace with God and my sexuality was by going to church and exorcising the demon that resided inside of me.

The fact that almost all of my neighbours were doing it too helped me to go ahead with it and I used the time to bond with them and create a relationship with them.

What I am about to write and share with you I swore I would never share with anyone, because I felt ashamed and disgusted by myself needlessly. I blamed myself for it all, when I now know it was just an act of miscommunication.

We started our weekly catechesis in April of 1999, and by June our Father had been transferred and a new one arrived. During this transition I had this burning desire to speak to someone, someone who could help me, and tell them about my dirty and sinful "secret."

So I thought: "This new priest doesn't know me and he cannot judge me, and this is killing me."

For the very first time in my entire life, at the age of 15, I felt valued and listened to and I felt like a "normal" person.

What happened as a result of this was that I created a fantasy in my head and he became a very important figure in my life for the next six months.

I was confused and, because someone gave me some attention, I thought I was in love with this priest. No one knew, just me and him, because the amount of time I started spending at church was much more than was required of me.

By now, I had already resigned myself and conformed and I knew nothing would EVER happen, for two reasons - he was straight and he was a celibate priest. So in my mind I had taken the decision to become a priest too, as soon as I finished high school.

It was resolute.

Final answer.

Although I still had feelings for him, I kept them to myself and hid them as well as I could. I wanted to make both our lives as easy as possible.

My memory fails me and I am not 100% sure if we did talk about it or not. If we did, we must have touched on it. If we didn't, then I thought I would let it fade away.

Either way, I completed my Holy Communion and confirmation. I continued to go to church pretty much on a daily basis. This was the only thing that could occupy me and keep me sane.

I had no life, nothing to do. All the books I had read, my encyclopaedias were about to scream at me and ask me to leave them alone, the Bible I had read and knew it pretty much by heart.

One Friday, 21st of January 2000, after having done some home visits for the less mobile, at around 11 am once our visits had finished, I went to church with the priest and just before I left I gave him a hug and said to him: "You are one of the best things that has ever happened to me in my entire life!"

I said nothing else. There was no malice in my words. Yes, these words came from love, but just love, universal and godly love - no lust, no ulterior motives.

I continued my week as normal. There was nothing to do, just count the days to go back to school, so I could graduate and become a priest.

On Saturday 29th of January, 8 days after my comment, during Mass, towards the end of the ceremony just before the Holy Communion, this priest looked at me in the eyes (I will never forget the intensity and redness of his eyes). He shook my hand and then he said: "Son, do not go and take the Holy Communion today."

I did as I was told, always did. I immediately grew curious and wanted to know the reason behind it. There had to be an explanation, surely.

To my amazement, I didn't need to wait any longer.

I was sitting on the first row, as I always did. On this occasion there weren't many people near me, I had 2-3 rows all for myself.

Then the announcements section came. This time he read the announcements. Normally it would be somebody else, this time he did it.

And it read as follows:

"From today on Jorge Vence will not be allowed the Holy Communion until further notice."

He didn't need to say anything else. I knew what had happened.

Years of practice at pretending allowed me to hold my head high while I was exiting the building. I could feel this almost primal desire to scream and cry but I didn't.

I went to a water fountain near his office in the hope of talking to him and confronting it, though all the doors were locked. They never were usually.

As I was about to walk towards the main exit, a friend came running towards me, hugged me and asked:

"Is everything OK?"

I burst into tears. This hug, and her presence in fact, were a godsend in that instance.

I never held on so tight to anyone. We walked with my face covered and got a taxi to her place.

We talked about what had happened. I explained everything. Thank God she believed me, otherwise I would have died of shame and embarrassment.

Because this friend had been part of the church for many years, she had built a particularly strong relationship with the previous priest, who was a dear friend of her family.

She said she had spoken to the previous priest, and he was going to help me, or at least talk about it.

The next day I left very early. I said to my mother I was going to visit a friend and I was going to be a while, not to worry about me.

My mother had already shown some concerns about the amount of time I was spending at church. She threatened to speak to the priest if I didn't stop going with such frequency. I decided to call her bluff.

So the next day when I set off to speak to my friend's priest friend, my mother decided to go to church (which she never did), and this time she was going to speak to the priest. So, toward the end of Mass she too heard the same announcement.

Just like me she waited to speak to him, and in this chat, where I was not present, he said to my mother:

"Your son had declared his love for me, and I did what was best for the both of us."

If now I could choose a word, I would probably choose 'blasphemy.' That is not the point here, though.

Later that day, after having had a lengthy chat with the other priest and as I was about to leave, to my surprise my mother was waiting for me outside the church. I have no idea how long she had been there, but she was there for me.

I wish I could say that was the easiest conversation I have had with my mother. If I did, I would be lying because it wasn't.

My mother found out about my sexual preferences in perhaps the worst possible scenario and I had no control or say in it.

One of the first things she said to me, when she greeted me, was:

"Ciao has died!"

Ciao was my cat. He was the most beautiful and caring cat I had ever owned. He was killed that morning and I had no tears left for him.

At that point, I asked what else could go wrong.

I would soon find out.

After this incident I continued to see my friend's priest. I needed that connection with God and religion.

So far, I have been open with you. I am telling you something that has been part of me and my life for just over half of my life, and not many people knew about this.

Before I continue with my story... I met another priest, a gentleman, whom I very dearly called "Dad", who manifested himself in my life in a very strange manner.

I had been to my cousin's church, because in all my confusion prior to the 21st of January I knew I wanted to speak to someone and confess. To my surprise the priest I intended to speak to was on holiday (Yes, priests take holidays too!).

So, this apparition of a gentleman stood in front of me and said: "Can I help you?" To which I said: "Oh, I am not sure, you are not the person I wanted to speak to." (How very rude!)

I honestly do not know what made me talk to him, but I am ever so glad I did. This gentleman was my rock for months. The love I got from him was that of a son of God, so pure and caring and supporting.

I was also seeing him alongside my friend's priest. I needed help and I wanted to be "normal." I would do whatever it took.

As weeks progressed and passed, the void in my heart grew bigger. And yes, you can guess, I had no confidence, no self-esteem. I had nothing left, I was a shell of a young man, a shell of a teenager.

My priest, who I will call Dad now, said to me: "I know of a psychiatrist who may help with any "trauma" you may need to address. Here is how you can get to her."

I took his advice, I always did.

At this particular moment, I want you to know that this gentleman, my Dad, restored any faith in humanity in me. He provided me with that belief in people, adding value in my life, making me want to be better and choosing to be better.

I went to see this lady psychiatrist. This was her volunteering work and she was very honest with me, and said: "You are out of my comfort zone. I do, however, know of someone who may help you."

So I took her advice and went to see the person, who was the leading professional working with gays in Panama City.

I turned up at this door, and we chatted. Unfortunately he couldn't see me either, because I was a minor, and they feared the other guys could negatively influence me or my decisions in life (how wrong they were!).

I was yet again referred elsewhere. This time I was sent to a psychology ward that specialised in minors, and there I started to see a psychologist and a psychiatrist - an hour at a time with each one of them.

By the way, all of this had happened in just 2 or 3 weeks. I was moving fast. I wanted to be "better," it had to happen quickly!

Because of my state I was advised to go on anti-depressants for a while, and continue to see them and my friend's priest too.

At first it sort of helped, I am not going to deny it. I was hurting and the pills were numbing my emotions and that was enough for me.

Sadly, my relationship with my mother had been scarred. She could not look me in the eyes. She proceeded to tell me how I had destroyed her dreams and that she once had me on a pedestal and now I was nothing.

I took those words in and said nothing back to her.

School had started so I had something to distract me. Needless to say, my peers could see a difference in me. They just didn't know what it was.

On Sunday 26th of March I found as much courage as I possibly could and I decided to visit the church from which I had been "kicked-out," knowing that the priest who had made the public announcement was due to be there.

I was nervous and anxious about visiting the church.

To my amazement, as soon as he noticed me there, he came to greet me and shook my hand as if nothing had ever happened. In fact, he welcomed me to take the Holy Communion if I so desired.

I held it all together and showed no "weakness." I was still dying inside, and at the same time I showed I was not a victim (I was not his victim – when, to be frank, I was!). I chose not to be his prisoner.

The next day, Monday 27th of March, I had the morning from hell. Absolutely everything seemed to be going against me. I had no willpower left, I had no light left in me. I was dead as it was - what was the point?

I got home around 1pm, I fed my brother and I thought long and hard.

There was no life for me, there was no future. I continued to think and I made my decision. I decided against life. Life showed me no respect or interest, why should I choose to live? Or why should I choose life altogether?

I then took all the anti-depressants out of their packaging. One by one I lined them up in front of me, all 47 of them. I looked at them and doubted if I could do it. I felt remorse (for a fraction of a second) and I grabbed a glass of water.

I held them all in my right hand, looking at them, thinking it is for the best. I had them all in my hand and without any hesitation I put them all in my mouth and drank the water.

Five hours passed. I had no idea what happened inside of me. Suddenly I was woken up by my mother, telling me off for not having done the grocery shopping.

I did what I did best in those days and pretended I was "fine," just tired.

As I went to the corner shop, I could not feel a thing. I was so high on the drugs that I felt I could fly. I then remembered I had given my word to a friend to help her with science. I helped with the subject matter and had some dinner, and went to bed again.

Why did it not work?

I was so "unlucky" that even trying to commit suicide was not working for me.

I was doomed to lead a life of despair and mediocrity, and be unhappy for the rest of my days.

I did not tell my mother what I had done.

One thing I can say is that, "metaphorically," my mother gave me life for a second time.

I do not know what would have happened had she not woken me up. I can only wonder.

The next day came. I woke up, got up and I was fine. No sickness, no symptoms - I was alive.

There was no doubt I was living still.

I needed to talk to someone, so I spoke to my biology teacher at school. She listened and comforted me and showed me so much support, like I never experienced before.

In the weeks that followed, I told my mother what I had done. I spoke to the psychologist and psychiatrist too, and together they came to the conclusion that I needed to see this expert (mentioned before), who was the leading professional working with gays - the one who couldn't see me because I was a minor.

All the formalities were dealt with and within a week or so I was ready for my first live group therapy.

These were the most inspiring and empowering Mondays of my entire life. I learned about wonderful people who, like me, thought life was against them, although they did have the support from one another to break old paradigms and overcome their false and limiting beliefs about life.

I can say that the day I officially made the choice to be better was on the 28th of March 2000. I said to life: "Listen, and listen carefully. You did your worst to get me down, but you didn't. Now it is my turn to take control of my life and show people what is possible - to overcome a 'living hell' and create the life you so deserve."

I continued going to the group therapy for around two years. I started attending at the age of 16 and stopped just after my 18th birthday.

Here, as I mentioned, I met wonderful men who supported me when I thought I had nothing left.

In here, the most valuable lesson I learned was that I am Jorge Vence. I am a son, a brother, a friend, a lover, a neighbour. I am many things and, by the way, I happen to be gay.

That message I never forgot, because words didn't define me. I defined myself.

Out of all of the wonderful men, I got really close to one in particular - my namesake, Jorge. He went out of his way to mentor and guide me. He was like an older brother, for that I am eternally grateful.

It is because of him that my life changed. My life was transformed for the best.

One Saturday night, on the 30th of December 2000, Jorge encouraged me to go out with him to a nightclub and celebrate my graduation. I had never been to a club, never mind with my mother letting me go.

After a row with my mother I escaped and ran for my life (the one I was granted for a second time!). I was shaking and trembling, I was beyond nervous.

It was this night I met the most incredible person, who saw me and healed many of my wounds, showing me love and respect and believed in me too. This night I met my Irish ex-partner, Donal Hogan.

When I saw him for the first time my heart stopped. There was a sense of acquaintance. I had seen him somewhere, but where I did not know.

It turns out that we had never met before.

Like in every good story we fell in love.

We had the best two months of my life. I went from wanting to be dead to fighting for a life with purpose and love.

Sadly he had to leave, which I knew would happen, but not that soon. I was left with a missing part. I had fallen in love and this love was saying goodbye to me now.

Again, you see my life has had its ups and downs, like many of you…

So, I got on with my life I was gaining control over. By now I was at university. I wanted to study medicine, I just didn't get the grades to get in. My second best option was biology.

Oh, you probably gathered that that thought of becoming a priest was long gone.

On the 13th of September 2001, two days after the 9/11 incident in the US, I received a call from an unknown number. It was him, my Donal. He got back in touch with me and reassured me he wanted a life with me. He asked if I wanted to come and visit him in England.

My response was a big, fat and ever so emphatic "Yes."

I came to visit him at the beginning of 2002. We chose to make it work, we talked and decided what we would do. I left England after two months and went back to Panama. I had a dream about the future.

We continued a long-distance relationship and by December of the same year I moved to England for good.

As they say, the rest is history. I was given a second chance for a reason. I was not sure what it was. I was just determined to find out, and that I certainly did.

After moving to England many wonderful memories were created. I took on various studies. I started working and enjoying my life.

My relationship with my Irish lover ended (in a very amicable manner, I must add – we are still really close friends!). I continued learning about myself and growing as a person and confident.

In August 2009 my life would change again for the best. On this occasion love decided to knock on my door and, when I least expected it, I met my rock, best friend, accomplice and inspiration, the person with whom I have truly Grown Confident, Martin MacKenzie.

Once my life was complete and whole again, I could see clearly what path I had to follow to help people in my life and in the world.

I then trained in applied psychology techniques and skills to empower people to be better and more and add value to their lives and everybody else's.

Now that you know my story, I firmly believe this can testify that it does not matter how hard you fall. What matters is how far you bounce back. I found strength and confidence I did not know I had and I was willing to give it a good shot.

This is why I was given a second chance, so you could read this story and be inspired by it.

Telling Your Story To The World: Things To Avoid

There is only one thing to avoid when you tell your story. Do not share a negative one.

Empower rather than discourage, ignite rather than put out a flame, breathe out life rather than hatred and be love.

Telling Your Story To The World: The Exercises

I have to admit I have been surprising myself with the exercises I have come up with so far. These ones aren't the exception.

1. Watch Your Social Media Contributions!

From now on, I advise you to take a look at what you say and how you say it online.

Are people feeling empowered by your message?

Also, take a look at your friends' message, and those who you follow.

Remember, choose to be better, as at times our emotions betray us and in the heat of the moment we want to tell the world. Just watch what you say on social media.

2. Write A Blog

This is so easy and inexpensive. Write about something you are really passionate about.

The world wants to hear your story, you just don't know it yet.

3. Write Poems

The poems you have been reading at the end of each step have been inspired by the content. At the same time I release my emotions on the paper while telling a story or my personal story.

Poetry is the song of the soul and this song resonates with many people at an emotional level. Share your passion and emotions with others.

4. Video Yourself

Yep, you are reading right!!!

Video yourself, especially in a social context. In this way you are able to observe how you interact with others when you communicate, see their reactions and yours too.

Do this once a month, and see if you notice any patterns in the way you communicate and the responses you get.

Do not forget, the meaning of communication is the response you get.

5. Continue Your Journal

This is the best way to track what story you tell yourself.

It upsets me to know that the tradition of keeping a diary has almost died out. I found it such a profound and beautiful way to revisit and review one's emotions and personal growth and evolution.

Journaling is like a keeping a diary. Let's just call it a "grown-ups" one.

Just write, write, write and find any patterns when you can.

Your mind is always doing its best to communicate with you. Journaling is the way to listen to it.

Keep doing it.

I Have A Story

How long have I been waiting for this moment?
How many lessons did I have to learn?
What did it have to undergo to stand in front of you?
My life was purposeless, for I had nothing to tell,
I had nothing to share, I was empty.
I just did not know it.
Now, I wake to the truth, I see the reality,
I am here for you,
I am here to tell you my truth.
I thought I had nothing to say, I was wrong,
I did not see the value of my word,
Now I do, and I want to tell, as much as I can.
Life is one, live it well.
Honour it, live it
Treasure it, share it.
I thought I had nothing to say, I thought wrong,
I see you, please listen to my story,
I too was lost, I too was wrong.
Life may seem chaotic at times,
Nothing seems to fits at all,
Be patient, wait, the time will come.
I believed I knew nothing, I was wrong,
Today here I am, in front of you,
Guiding you, nurturing you.
I do have a life, worth living and fighting for,
I have a message, I do have a story,
Listen, do pay attention.
You needn't worry, you needn't hurry,
Life will be on your side, that much I know.
Live, love, just be.
Listen and pay attention,
I do have a story, please pay attention.
You needn't worry, you needn't hurry.
When the time is right and the lessons learned,
You too will have a story,
Till then my friend, you needn't hurry, you needn't worry.

Step 9: Sharing Your Gift With The World

"The greatest gift that you can give to others is the gift of unconditional love and acceptance."

Brian Tracy

The purpose of this step is to help you find ways in which you can share your gift with the world and make a real difference in people's lives.

No matter what anyone says, we all have something to share that is unique to us and can make a difference in the world, be it a talent, a skill, or a special message we want to tell the world.

This step goes hand in hand with telling your story to the world. Your gift could well be that. There are countless people who have done just that and have added value to millions of people by their act of courage, bravery and confidence.

A lot of people have the misconception that a gift has got to be something physical, with a monetary value attached to it. This is far from the truth. A musician shares his gift with his music, an artist shares his gift with his paintings, a poet shares his gift through his poetry, a chef shares his gift with his food, etc.

What is that "something" you are so good at, that by sharing it with the world you can make a remarkable difference?

If you are like I used to be, you may be saying to yourself: "I have nothing to share with the world. I am not good at anything."

Well, let me tell you, this is inaccurate.

You have got something to share.

You and only you have something so special in you that, once you recognise what it is, you will naturally and effortlessly share it with everyone.

You know you are sharing your gift with others when they compliment you on what you do.

What is it most people compliment you on?

Are you a caring person?

Are you a generous person?

Are you a great listener?

Are you an entertainer?

Are you an animal lover?

Are you a plant lover?

Do you care for the environment?

As you can see, there are endless ways in which you are able to share what you do or who you are with others.

I will share with you something I once did in order to figure out what I was good at or what people thought I was good at.

I simply asked people, especially those nearest and dearest to me. Here is what I did.

I said to my friends at high school: “Hey guys, I am really concerned about my future and I would like to know what I am really good at. Could you please help me?”

I then handed them a questionnaire. Don’t be too scared, it was only 5 questions.

1. What do you think of me?
2. What am I good at?
3. What do other people think about me?
4. What do others say I am good at?
5. What do you think my ideal job could be?

At this point I want to clarify that what others thought of me did not define me. The same applies to you. What others think of you does not define you.

The objective or reason behind these questions was to find out what areas I needed to improve or get better at (in order to be better and add value, all through curiosity!), and use their feedback to construct a profile of what I may be really good at.

My friends’ answers were so honest and humbling. I was expecting them to be critical, negative or dishonest.

To my surprise this is what they all said: “You are a good friend, a good listener, you are intelligent and you are able to simplify even the most complex of concepts so it is understood by everyone.”

I was blown away by the kindness and honesty in their words.

I highly recommend you give this a go and be open to people’s feedback.

Another way to tap into your gift is to go back to a memory as a child and remember what it is you wanted to do when you grew up. What was your calling as a child?

In my case I always felt this attraction toward medicine and psychology. I understood the importance of being healthy, both physically and mentally. That was my childhood dream.

If you can’t remember what you wanted to be or do when you were a child, ask your family and friends. I am sure they will have tales to tell.

Please do not let the fact that you aren’t clear about your gift (just yet!) get you worked up or disappointed. I too found myself in that situation for a few years. I went from wanting to become a priest, to wanting to do medicine, then to studying biology, then to learning gastronomy, then to studying management and leadership, so I could then find my true passion and gift.

I strongly encourage you to take a look at your journal. You may have been writing one prior to reading this book. Look for clues and ideas there. What thoughts keep repeating?

Keep your mind open and when you least expect it, it will become apparent and obvious to you what your gift to the world is.

Time is not only the best healer, but the best ally we could ever have. As long as we give it time and open our minds and hearts to it, all the answers we ever looked for and sought for years come to us.

Sharing Your Gift: My Story

I am confident you may have gathered by now what my gift to the world is.

You are holding it in your hands. You have been learning from it and at the same time Growing Confident, becoming better and adding value to your life.

Since I have been honest and open with you, it is only suitable to tell you how I came to write this book.

From a very early age I loved books. I devoured them. When I started high school I was fortunate enough to have a very passionate Spanish tutor. She lived and breathed our language.

So, literature and poetry were the best avenues to learn and explore our incredible language.

This passionate tutor infused and passed on her passion to me and other peers.

When I moved to the UK I had plenty of time on my hands, so it felt pertinent and appropriate to dedicate my time to writing, which I did. Since my fears and doubts got the better of me, neither my poems nor my fiction-book ever saw the light of day.

I buried that thought deep in the abyss of my mind and occasionally it would pop out and haunt me for a few minutes.

On several occasions I would get the manuscript out and I would start editing it, and these doubts and fears would invade me again.

I did this several times, my fiction-book and poems alike. You would have thought that the fact that I was writing in Spanish would make me more comfortable with proceeding, but it just didn't.

Although life, as it happens, "got in the way" of many things and I forgot about it completely, my passion and desire to read and learn new things never faded. If anything it just got stronger.

On many occasions I would hear and read: "We all have a book in us, waiting to come out!" To which "the voice in my head" would reply: "You have been waiting long enough!"

During this growth I was undergoing, my learning and curiosity for life, I met several people who had written books.

My goodness, everyone has written a book and none of them has been published!!!

Hearing this would make me panic and undervalue what I had to offer. I made the mistake many people make, which was to compare myself to others. I would say to myself: "If X or Y (who are better than me) can't get a book published, that means I have no chance in hell to even get near a publisher!"

This thought continued to discourage me for months and even years.

To be 100% honest with you, I had resigned myself to the idea that I would never ever, not in this life, be writing a book again, let alone publishing it.

I will complete the book story in a short while, I promise. To be continued…

Part of my gift is the set of skills, knowledge and techniques I gained along the way.

You remember me telling you that as I child I wanted to be and dreamed of becoming a doctor (before wanting to become a priest that was!), and specialise in psychiatry. It was very clear in my head.

Things happened, as they always do. Or, to use my mentor Silvia's language, events occurred, most of which were unknowable events. (Please refer to Silvia's book, 'Events Psychology,' 2009, Dragon Rising Publishing.)

I always believed things happened for a reason and I still do.

So, as mentioned, I went from career to career, learning "stuff," some of which would enrich my life, some other "wasted" my time (or so I thought!).

One day I found myself learning about Leadership and Management. It was here that I discovered that desire to care for and empower others.

During my time at college I had to carry out a project using Leadership and Management skills. I decided to focus on "Staff Performance at Work." My findings were shocking. The vast majority of the staff/employees were underperforming for one reason only - low self-esteem and lack of confidence!!!

As a direct result they were not meeting the company's expectations, and to make matters even worse, they were not receiving the training required to empower them and "lift their spirits."

This was a decisive moment in my life, as I took the decision to train and become a vessel of empowerment, so every person I met could also Grow Confident and achieve their full potential.

Needless to say, I trained in Life Coaching, NLP, EFT, Matrix Re imprinting, CBT (Cognitive Behavioural Therapy), Reiki, Modern Stress Management and Project Sanctuary.

I have touched the lives of many, and I am ever so grateful for what I get to do, though I am only getting started.

You may be asking yourself: "And what about the book?"

This came to be by accident. On a beautiful weekend in Eastbourne, England, I invested in myself and personal development and took the decision to train in Project Sanctuary, an advanced energy technique designed and mastered by Silvia Hartmann.

What I learned in those three days was to work with my unconscious mind, the true and real mastery of the self, of the emotions and real energy work.

I remember making a comment to Silvia, about wanting to write a book. It is worth noting that Silvia has published umpteen books and her writing is flawless and to the point.

The moment I read Silvia it was love at first read.

I was honoured to just be there learning from her. Silvia, being the generous and abundant person she is, shared with me and other peers all she knew.

So, we started coming up with book ideas, using her magic symbols, derived from Project Sanctuary too.

By Sunday 21st of June 2015, I didn't just have one book idea, but 23!!!

I went from believing I could never write a book, to believing I could write all 23. I was on a roll, ideas could not stop coming into my head and I felt in control, again!

We shortlisted our ideas. 23 went down to 15, 15 down to 9, 9 down to 5, 5 down to 3, 3 down to 2, and I had two finalists. I had to choose between Guiding Stars or Growing Confident.

I stood up looking at both ideas. I could see them clearly in my head – in my mind's eye. I just had to choose one and, almost without knowing what I was doing, I chose Growing Confident.

I let my inner guidance system take control and lead me to the best title, the one that would help the most people and at the same time would allow me to learn more about myself.

Within 10 minutes I had a complete draft of what I was going to do. I had a deadline and, most importantly, I was to be made accountable for this book seeing the light of day.

So here it is - my gift to you. Empowerment, control, choices, life, love, hope, belief, optimism and the opportunity to start afresh. It is simple, and you only need to let it happen.

It is just a matter of following these 9 simple steps so far. The 10th is equally as important, it just derives from practising the 9 you have learned so far:

- Choose to be better - add value to people's lives,
- Curiosity - see life through the eyes of a child,
- Healing the past - letting go of imprisonment from the self,
- Learning from the past - mastery of one's past,
- Modelling - learning from others' skills and techniques,
- Acting as if - borrowing someone else's belief and making it your own,
- Being open - mastering one's emotions,
- Telling the world your story - saying boldly this is me, this who I am,
- Sharing your gift with the world - saying this is me, this is what I have to offer.

Please do not underestimate these simple, yet powerful steps. They helped me and have helped many others.

What do you have in you that is unique and special? Discover it and share it with as many people as you possibly can.

Sharing Your Gift: Things To Avoid

This is perhaps the briefest advice I could give you so far. Do not deprive the world of what you have to offer. It matters (you matter!), it will add value to the rest of the population and it is your birthright, so honour it and share it.

Sharing Your Gift: The Exercises

1. Ask Others What They Think Of You

Ask your friends and family the following questions:

1. What do you think of me?
2. What am I good at?
3. What do other people think about me?
4. What do others say I am good at?
5. What do you think my ideal job could be?

Find a quiet and appropriate time and ask them if they would mind doing you a favour.

Explain that you are doing a self-discovery exercise and for this it is required that people you love answer the above questions.

A word of advice: what they say does not define you, it is only feedback. You remember earlier, when I mentioned the NLP presuppositions? One of them says: "There is no such thing as failure, only feedback."

It does not matter how positive or negative their comments and feedback are. What matters is how you interpret it and what you can learn from it. Remember, you are in control of your life.

I highly recommend you to ask at least 10 people, or more if you can.

2. The "My Gifts" Competition

Make a list of possible career paths and ways in which you could share your gift with the world. What are your strengths in life? How can you positively impact the lives of others?

Make a very thorough list, and then shortlist them, then further and further, until only one remains. You can think of it as a beauty pageant where only the best and most beautiful go through to the next round, until the winner is crowned!

First Round

1. ______________________________
2. ______________________________
3. ______________________________
4. ______________________________
5. ______________________________
6. ______________________________
7. ______________________________
8. ______________________________
9. ______________________________
10. ______________________________
11. ______________________________
12. ______________________________
13. ______________________________
14. ______________________________
15. ______________________________
16. ______________________________
17. ______________________________
18. ______________________________
19. ______________________________
20. ______________________________
21. ______________________________
22. ______________________________
23. ______________________________

Second Round

1. ____________________
2. ____________________
3. ____________________
4. ____________________
5. ____________________
6. ____________________
7. ____________________
8. ____________________
9. ____________________
10. ____________________
11. ____________________
12. ____________________

Quarter Final

1. ____________________
2. ____________________
3. ____________________
4. ____________________
5. ____________________
6. ____________________
7. ____________________
8. ____________________

Semi Final

1. ____________________
2. ____________________
3. ____________________
4. ____________________

Final

1. ____________________
2. ____________________

And The Winner Is ...

1. ____________________

3. Take Action

Give of your time to others. We have already talked about giving to charity.

This time you can do the same or, even better, volunteer some of your time to work in charities or your community, at school, etc.

There are so many ways in which you can give your time to other people and share the gift of you with them.

Become a lighthouse in the darkness of someone's life. And that's all about doing something positive, by taking action.

I believe by now you have a well-formed idea of what it is you want to give to the world, your gift.

Just a few things to bear in mind.

- This has to be positive and impact people positively,
- It has to be important to you,
- Give yourself a deadline,
- Find an accountability buddy, someone to whom you will give your word and they will make sure you see it through,
- Create an action plan and a strategy.

The key to make your dreams come true and, in this case, to share your gift with the world is to TAKE ACTION, right now.

Accept My Gift

I have travelled the distance,
I have seen the sights,
My life is the evidence,
For I have learned,
I have lived and loved.
Today, here I stand,
With all there is and all I have,
My dearest, my darling,
Here I am, for you,
Please take my hand.
Accept my gift.

Step 10: Living Love

"We are born of love; love is our mother."
Rumi

This step is about putting it altogether, Growing Confident and living love, not only in yourself but with everyone in your life.

Why entitle this step "Living Love" ..?

The answer is perhaps the easiest to all the questions asked in this book so far.

How could there be confidence without love?

I sat here, wondering what to say next. How can I inspire you even further, so you see fast and lasting results?

Let me start by asking you a question.

What made you pick this book or buy this e-book?

What was the reason behind it?

What did you intend to get from this book?

While you gather your thoughts and allow your mind to settle and give you the answers you seek for, this is what we have learned so far.

In order to Grow Confident: (in case you were wondering, I chose the word 'growing' because we are organic matter. Everything about us is based on natural reactions, so 'growing' I found appropriate. This what I did, please accept this, my gift to you.)

The Ten Steps To Growing Confident

1. **Choose to be better - don't wish things were different; wish you were better, add value to your life and the lives of many others.**
2. **Curiosity - be curious about everything, cross-examine life the way a child does, see life through the eyes of a child.**
3. **Healing the past - letting go of unwanted and negative memories is the healthiest thing any person can do, so you can move forward and create the life you deserve.**
4. **Learning from the past - healing and letting go of the past needn't be painful or hurtful. You can revisit the past and learn from it, so you don't remain its prisoner.**
5. **Modelling - watch and learn from people, model their excellence, borrow their belief.**
6. **Acting as if - just like modelling, borrow someone's belief and make it yours, so that by practising and repetition it can be yours too.**
7. **Being open - when you are exposed and vulnerable, the real magic happens. People see the real you and you can say you have made mistakes and that you are human too!**
8. **Telling your story to the world - what you know and have matters, so why not share it with as many people as you can?**
9. **Sharing your gift with the world - you possess talents and skills nobody else on this planet has. This is your gift, share it with the world.**
10. **Living love - this is when you put everything together and you discover your purpose. You realise you have Grown Confident not for you, but for humanity's sake, to empower and inspire the masses, to live and to love, to be, to have and to do, to honour your life and break free from the imprisonment of yesteryears and head toward your full potential, toward the real you!**

This book has taught me that what really gave me the strength and confidence to get up and fulfil my mission in life is love, was love, has always been love and will continue to be love.

I realise that when I was at my lowest I lacked love, and this love wasn't the love you would expect from others, but from myself. I lacked self-love.

Life taught me many lessons and each one of these lessons built on from the previous one, and each time I would get closer to my self-discovery and mastery.

As a teenager, like many of us do, I thought my "problems" were bigger than the rest, that there was no solution to what I was going through and life was against me.

Now, I know better.

We have lived trapped in a prison created by ourselves to protect us from hurt and pain and agony and solitude. Sadly this prison, this man-made, imaginary prison, backfired on us and did the complete opposite.

Many generations have been swimming upstream, fighting the current, not knowing otherwise. It just seemed safer.

No-one taught our ancestors and forefathers what was possible, that we had the tools needed to overcome our obstacles, that all we ever needed was already inside of us.

If they had listened to their inner guidance, they would have found those resources a lot sooner, passed it on to their offspring and to the generations to come, healing the wounds and giving room to options, choices and possibilities.

We see it in children. They know no fear, they know no limits, although the very first word they hear is "NO" and the very first word they speak is "NO" (or at least one of the first words!).

Are we conditioning and limiting ourselves from achieving our full potential?

For what purpose?

Have we not gone through enough so far? Or do we want more? Because quite frankly we have not learned our lessons.

Growing Confident is much more than gaining strength and courage and power or control. Rather the opposite - it is to be, to be open, to be truthful and honest, to be willing and accepting.

Growing Confident isn't easy, nor is it difficult.

Growing Confident comes from the desire of being better, making a decision to make a difference and see it through.

Growing Confident is what you and I deserve, it is our birthright. We just did not know it.

Growing Confident is truly living love, living in love, living with love, living loved, living for love, living loving and loving living.

When I started writing this book I thought I knew what I was going to write. I was wrong.

Yes, there was a structure. I had a vague and faint idea of what I was going to be writing about and in the end my inner guidance, my intuition, took over and wrote what had to be written.

I stopped questioning what I was writing. Instead I decided to allow it and let it see the light of day, and write the language that you could understand so you could benefit even more.

Have I accomplished what I had set out to do?

The answer is NO.

I accomplished much more. I opened my heart and let love guide my every keystroke. I let my heart speak in the language of love, because yes, I may have never met you and I just know I feel such love for you, because you are the reason I am writing these words. You are the reason I Grew Confident, so I could fight my own fears and destroy the prison I created and which held me captive for many years. You are the reason I freed myself from my own imprisonment. You are the reason I exist.

Life threw many things in my direction, at me, and I just realised it was life, because life is love and love is life. I am the one who allowed my emotions and past to control and rule over my life. I just didn't know it.

Now I know, whether I move forward or not, it is my choice. I decide what I do, what I eat, what I wear, not out of rebellion, but because I know I am in charge and my life goes the way I decide it to go.

When I sat in front of the black screen, I almost fled and let my limiting beliefs overtake me. This time I was ready to fight, for I had love on my side, and nothing was going to make me crumble.

The first word was a struggle, the second had some resistance and now I am typing at such speed, only because the truth wants to come out.

It is time you too start living, it is time you too start loving.

So far, you may think it is all about me and my story. Well it isn't, because you and I are one and the same. I Grow Confident and so do you; you Grow Confident, so do I.

I have learned that Growing Confident is a win-win scenario, because quite frankly there are no losers in life. We all win, we just don't know it.

All of this is about to stop, because you and I are waking up. And together we are not only stronger, but we can reach the lives of thousands, if not millions, of people.

The day I was given a second chance, you too were given a second chance. I had a story to share, and that prophecy has been fulfilled. I have told you my story and given you my gift. It is your turn now.

What steps will you take now?

Do you know enough?

Is there anything missing?

What else should I add next time, so you Grow even more Confident?

What I have learned over the last 3 decades of my life has been personal to me. I felt I had to share with you, so you too could wake up to your true self, to your excellence and perfect state.

If you take the first step and choose to be better, that is 10% of your journey to Growing Confident.

May you add your curiosity to choosing to be better. That is an additional 10%. You are 20% of the way there, and that is a lot closer than many ever get.

Healing the past would add a further 10%, and if you learn from the past that is another 10%. You are 40% of the way there…

Imagine what your life will be like by improving by 40%.

When you add modelling and acting as if into your life, you are adding another 20%. That is more than half way to 100%. Those who get to 60% consider themselves lucky and fortunate to have overcome their limitations and negative beliefs. Yet there is much more to achieve and be done.

You then start being open. This puts you much further down the road to mastery than the world has ever seen, than your world has ever seen!

So then you start telling the world your story, who you are.

This is me, this is all I am, this is all I have. Take me or leave me, though with me you are stronger and better.

Now you are at 80%. Can you imagine what this means to your life, your friends and family and the planet itself?

Then, your gift is revealed to you, and you honour it and share it with men, women and children alike, so you touch their lives with what only you can give to the world.

My, oh my, we are at 90%, so close, so near and yes, it is possible, it is attainable.

What else do we need to make a 100%?

What can we add to round it up?

What is missing in this equation, so that by adding this magical ingredient everything falls into place and the world is transformed and you have fully Grown Confident and mastered your emotions and life?

"Fully mastered?" I can hear some of you screaming.

The answer is yes.

I have learned and understood that nothing can ever get you and bring you down when you are in control of your emotions, state and life.

When you make a mistake, rather than dwelling on it for years or even decades, you say out loud and proudly: "I messed up, so what? What can I learn from it? How will this enrich my life?"

How empowering is this response?

If something "bad" happens in your life, rather than getting upset about it and letting it hold you back and hinder you in life, look at it in the eyes and say: "I see you. I know you are teaching me a lesson. Bring it on, show me it and let me move forward."

What is that saying? "When life gives you lemons, make lemonade."

Wow. Can you see yourself responding like this in the future?

Growing Confident and mastery only occur and happen when you open your heart, you let go of the past, you forgive yourself and everybody else, and wave goodbye to it, brush yourself off and walk toward the future.

Love is the key ingredient that glues it all together.

On one occasion my mother confided something really personal to her, which at the moment of hearing it made me feel very upset for her and her ancestors: "Son," she said, "No-one ever taught me how to love."

I understand what my mother meant that day. No-one ever teaches us how to love. We are almost expected to automatically learn without any tutorial in the subject matter.

Now I know that love comes from within. Once it is nurtured and fed with positivity and kindness and beautiful thoughts, it can grow and flower and blossom and spread its seeds across the universe, travelling across time and matter and no force can destroy it.

Love is so pure and universal that it can survive anything, even our lack of understanding about it.

So, my message to you is:

Grow Confident
with love,
in love, for love.

I love you.

Living Love: My Story

By now, I have almost said everything I had to say. Love is my first priority, love is my second priority. In fact, love is my only priority.

It has been with love that I was able to grow strong, for without it I was numb and dormant.

I found love on the 28th of March 2000 when I woke up to my mission in this life, to tell you my story and share my gift with you.

As time went by this love grew stronger and so did my confidence.

After having attempted to end my life I found love, real love, not because it was a pity love but because I had learned to love myself. And this love was so powerful and strong it could only possibly attract more love into my life.

Love changed and transformed my life for the better. I grew up with lack and precarious conditions and because I said "Yes" to life and love, I was rewarded with abundance and prosperity.

I chose to be better, and love followed. I was curious and I found love. I healed the past and I uncovered love. I learned from the past and I learned to love myself and the world. I modelled excellence and acted as if I had all I ever wanted in life, and love came my way every single time. I was open and I was loved. I told my story to the world and love told me its story. I shared my gift with you and the world and love shared itself with me.

Love, love and more love.

I made the best friends anyone could ever wish for, because I had love in me - so much that it had to be shared.

Now I have the most loyal, loving, caring and wonderful partner. And why? Because I was love, I am love and I will continue to be love.

I choose love time and time again, over and over again. Even if I had to leave everything behind, I would follow love to the end of time.

I Grew Confident because I loved - because I loved myself first.

Today I wake up each and every single day feeling such love and giving myself love, because I know it is all I need to make it in life.

Confidence stems from love, and love is confidence.

It took me a few years to come to this conclusion and I am glad I did.

Let's celebrate love together and, as we do so, let's Grow Confident and become better people together, hand in hand, in love, living love.

Living Love: The Exercises

I could not come to this point and not set up some exercises.

1. Love Yourself

Stand in front of a mirror first thing in the morning as well as last thing at night and say out loud:

I LOVE MYSELF

I AM LOVE

I DESERVE LOVE

LOVE IS ALL THERE IS

I AM LOVE, I LOVE, I AM LOVED

I LOVE, THEREFORE I AM!

2. Love A Past Aspect

Think of a past aspect of you who needed someone to love them. Imagine they are standing before them. Tell them how much you love them from your heart.

3. Write A Love Letter To A Future You

Write a love letter to a future aspect, a future you. Think about the future aspect of you, who they are when they will read your letter. Mark in your diary when the letter should be read, about one month from now. Until then, put it somewhere safe where your future aspect will find it when the time has come.

4. Write A Love Letter To Someone You Love

Write a love letter to someone and deliver it to them by hand.

5. Share Love With Others

Tell everybody you meet that you love them.

Say it with pride:

"I LOVE YOU"

Love is nothing to be ashamed of.

6. Make Love Your Number 1 Priority.

You And I Are Living Love

I was born believing in the Promised Land,
So, early in my infancy I left,
Looking for a clue, chasing for the truth.
Oh I fell, and I hurt.
The road was lonely, the wind so cold.
I faced the wild, I felt the vile.
Oh I cried, and I survived.
Life taught me lessons,
So I listened and paid attention,
The roads were not for the faint hearted
So I learned with intention.
Oh I learned, and I converted,
To a believer and a teacher.
Here I am, walking with strength,
Knowing I am my own creator,
I have love and I have faith.
No need to cry, no need to fly
The coast is clear, no more fear,
Life is now on my side,
So now I know what I am here for,
To inspire and to propel you,
I am here to protect you,
No more hurt, no more pain,
Only life, only gain,
For you and I together in this game are,
No losers, only winners
Together you and I, hand in hand,
Growing, evolving,
Growing wise,
Growing old,
Growing strong,
Growing Confident,
Each day, some more,
So life for you and I
Is more meaningful
So you and I are living love.

Growing Confident: In Conclusion

By now you may have started to go on your own journey of growth and evolution, so I would like to highlight a few key things I think are worth sharing.

Real growth takes place only when you share it with others. Growing Confident isn't about you, it never has been. It is about everybody else… and love.

Confidence is about helping others, empowering them to see their real potential and overcome their fears, limitations and obstacles.

Being confident is having off-days, and feeling doubtful and fearful because it is in our DNA. The real evidence is when you say to yourself: "It is OK to feel this way and I will get on with what I want to do. I will just do it anyway."

Being confident isn't about wealth or riches. On the contrary, it is about being humble and true to your roots, to who you are, a loving being.

Real confidence isn't about strength. Far from it - it is about being soft and open and approachable.

You will have noticed that, when you follow the 10 simple steps described in this book, many concepts and ideas you may have had in the past about confidence will be in a way challenged and may even seem too straightforward and easy. Trust me, it is.

Confidence, I learned, is when you do your enjoyable best and as you do so, you also care and have in mind other people's emotions. You become mindful, respectful and you would not do unto others what you would not like done to you.

It is simple things like this that become so apparent and obvious, that you end up saying to yourself (out loud!): "Why did I not do this before?"

I believe you have found this book and most of its content (if not all!) of great help to you and everybody in your life.

We grow up being undermined and pushed, so confidence leaves our lives very early on.

To make matters a lot worse, one of the first words we learn is NO, which then becomes negative feelings, emotions and decisions about the world around us.

We forget that we are beings of love and strength, that our sole purpose is to live a life of joy and happiness, while adding value to the lives of each and every person in our life.

As children the light that once shone bright, so bright that it could put any star to shame, is put out and we grow insecure, doubtful, anxious and fearful - to name but a few.

As teenagers we "think" life is against us (at least I did). We are in a limbo, trapped in between generations and we want our voices heard, yet it seems an impossible task.

So, as adults we forget what it was like to be confident. Life gets in the way - work, family, society, etc.

Now that you have finally Grown Confident, go out there and share it with the world. Remember, life gets better when we help and love others.

Growing Confident was a journey, not because I became a better person, but because I made the decision to share with you how to Grow Confident too, so your life can be the life you always wanted.

Love,

Jorge

26/8/15

Southampton, Hampshire

Appendix 1: Modelling Your Own Excellence

You remember we covered modelling in Step 5, from an NLP approach. Now I think it is time we look at another approach to modelling.

This is so much simpler and more natural to do (in case you struggled with modelling someone else's excellence).

All you have to do is remember a time when you were 100% confident in yourself (remember what it was) and relive that experience and engage all of your senses as you do so.

When you do this, rerun it in your head - what you did, how you did it, where you did it, when you did it.

You will notice that as you remember and run through the memory you are able to discover the strategy you used in that particular instance, and by using it again you can get similar results (if not better!).

The more you model your own excellence, the better you get at discovering your own strategies for success and confidence and your own inner strength.

Also, you can explore how you will feel in a future situation, by doing a similar exercise.

Just close your eyes and imagine the future event. How are you feeling, what are you seeing, where are you, who is there?

Make a mental note of your physiology and confidence levels.

Are you 100% happy with what you are seeing? Is there something missing?

Mentally rehearse this, until you are 100% satisfied. Then write down the strategy you discovered and use it when necessary.

Do this exercise whenever you want to improve your state or results. You can equally learn from the past or the future, so as long as you bring it to the now and start working on it.

Note. This approach to modelling is gentler and kinder to you, because you are comparing your excellence to your own, so you can't fall in to the vicious circle of thinking that he/she is better than me.

Appendix 2: Living Confidence

Being confident is like being on top of your game, at whatever you do - no exception.

I decided to make an insert on Living Confidence.

What it is you can do when you live confidently?

The answer is plain and simple.

YOU CAN DO ANYTHING YOU WANT!

The day I woke up and noticed I had let go of my fears and doubts, I also realised I was able to do anything and everything I wanted.

I only needed to have a laser beam focus, a strategy and a vision to make it happen.

On one occasion when I was at college, just after I arrived in the UK, I entered a cookery competition. I was the only one of the delegates from our college to win a medal. It was a Silver medal in the Vegetarian category.

Soon after I received my medal, one of my peers made a cutting and sarcastic comment (which I did not know how to take!). She said: "You always have to be better than everybody else at whatever you do."

I was gob smacked for various reasons. I didn't know how to respond, I was expecting more support and lastly, I felt uncomfortable as to how my success affected others.

Now, when I look back, I am able to understand why I came across that way… I was a few years older than my peers (around 5 years). I had experiences they hadn't had yet (at the time) and I was spending quite a bit of money on my education, so I had to make it work.

The reason I have shared this story with you is because when you are confident, you should not care what others say about your successes and/or failures. If you do your best, your enjoyable best, and have fun at what you do, people's comments should not matter.

During my training to become a practitioner and trainer I learned the most from my peers - how to be open and honest, to trust in myself and to be confident at whatever I did, no matter what the outcome was.

Living Confidence is about acceptance, forgiveness, non-attachment, love, fun, happiness, joy and growth.

You can't evolve if you don't grow and learn from your experiences.

Please note how I said, experiences. There are no positive or negative experiences, there are only experiences. It is us and others who make them so, define them and carry their burden with us.

Living Confidence is waking up, looking at yourself in the mirror and saying out loud: "You are awesome! Today is the day I give the world the best of me!"

So, when you leave your house to get on with the day ahead, you have fired yourself up with positives and empowerment. And when those "negative" comments, people, things come to you, you are able to look at them and say: "You don't have control over me - go away."

Living Confidence is smiling at people and making them feel special, valued, wanted and appreciated.

In Reiki there are 5 principles by which I lead my life. These are:

- Just for today I will let go of anger
- Just for today I will let go of worry
- Today I will count my many blessings
- Today I will do my work honestly
- Today I will be kind to every living creature

Isn't this an incredible way to go about in life?

Just for today…

One day at a time… I don't worry about tomorrow, it is about today (working toward a better tomorrow, obviously).

Here we are able to see and identify qualities and principles worth exercising: non-attachment (remember the Aspects Model?), not living in fear or worry, gratitude, adding value to humanity and RESPECT.

Respect, I have learned, is key in Living Confidently. It doesn't matter how confident you are - if you don't respect others, they will not value what you have to offer if you mistreat them.

Quite frankly, respect and love go together hand in hand.

Let's not forget gratitude - being grateful for having good health, a roof over our heads, a job, food on our tables, family and friends etc., and also for being confident, and free from "our own prison."

Living Confidence isn't about what confidence and being confident mean to you, but how it can impact the life of others.

Do not forget, being and Growing Confident is NOT about you.

When you realise that being and Growing Confident is about others, the better life gets and the more you can do to help others.

So, go out there and share your confidence with the world, tell your story and gift to humanity.

Appendix 3: Empowering Others

This area of Growing Confident was a real turning point for me. The day I started empowering others to also Grow Confident, I felt I had started to make a real difference in the world.

This unit is mainly and mostly to stress the impact we have on other people's lives. Whether we want it or not, we are ROLE models to someone.

Each and every one of us is either someone's older brother, sister, cousin, neighbour, parent, uncle, auntie, in authority etc.

So then, why not choose daily to empower and have a positive impact on someone's life?

Have you ever been in a situation where you help someone in a difficult situation, and it is the moment they look at you and give you a heartfelt "Thank you," that you feel you have done something incredible - so incredible that you don't expect anything in return.

Imagine, for one second only, if you did this daily to more than one person. What positive impact would you have, not only on that person but on their families, colleagues and friends? And these people in return did the same with their families, colleagues and friends? Can you see that ripple effect of love, niceness and confidence?

What can you do from now on, so that you empower everyone you meet?

Perhaps you already do - congratulations!

How many more can you help and empower?

On one occasion I read a book entitled 'The five secrets you must discover before you die' by John Izzo. In this book the author tells the story of his grandfather who would tell him about being positively tired, having done the best he could for his friends and family during his day.

What a beautiful way to go about your day, helping people out at all moments of the day and sleeping restfully, like a log or a baby (depending on your preference), knowing you did the best you could for that day.

Then do the exact same the day after, and the next and the next, until it becomes a pandemic and everyone is doing the same…

Don't you think that empowering people this way would put an end to those things we know about and see and read on the news daily?

Just imagine, people being polite to one another and helping one another without expectations.

I firmly believe that that is 100% possible in our lifetime. We just have to be a role model and teach others to do the exact same, so the next generation will already have it as part of their *modus operandi*.

When you are confident - and let me be clear confident, not arrogant or egotistic - you cannot help but to care about others and their well being, because you know (a knowing some call awareness) that your strength has the power to help and improve the lives of hundreds, if not thousands.

Those thousands in return do the same with other thousands. Just imagine that compounded effect, and in the end a confident, loving, caring society with mutual respect and where everyone's views and opinions matter and no-one tries to outdo or outshine the other.

I invite you to take a good look around you and notice who is under your influence. How do you make them feel? Is there room for improvement? If so, what are you waiting for?

There are countless ways in which we can empower and inspire people. Just bear in mind what your gift is and use your talents to empower people.

I can give you my example. The way I empower people is through my work and training, cooking and entertaining, and now through this book.

How can you empower your closest circle of friends?

How can you empower your family?

How can you empower your colleagues?

Be part of their evolution and journey as they Grow Confident.

This is where the real wealth and abundance lie. You will be leaving a legacy that will outlive you and at the same time change the world for the better, even when you are long gone!

I encourage you to go out there and start empowering everyone you meet, plant the seed of confidence that will grow into beautiful, capable, empowered, loving and confident beings.

Appendix 4: My Favourite Energy Techniques

The information I am about to share with you I have been using in the last 2 years or so, and what it has done for me and in my life is beyond my words.

These energy raising techniques originate from EFT (Emotional Freedom Techniques), and have been evolved by Silvia Hartmann and then become Positive EFT, Energy EFT (Master Practitioner), Project Sanctuary and MSM (Modern Stress Management) – Stress to Success.

What they all have in common is ENERGY and not just any energy but our own energy, which is the greatest fountain of happiness, joy, success, accomplishment, wealth, health and love.

The SUE Scale

The SUE Scale (Subjective Units of Experience, from Events Psychology, Hartmann 2009) is an instrument designed to measure the level of energy flow through the energy body from -10 to +10. It replaces the SUD Scale (Subjective Units of Distress, Wolpe 1969) as a measure to express how a person is feeling/what they are experiencing and represents a paradigm shift in the treatment of stress and emotional disturbances.

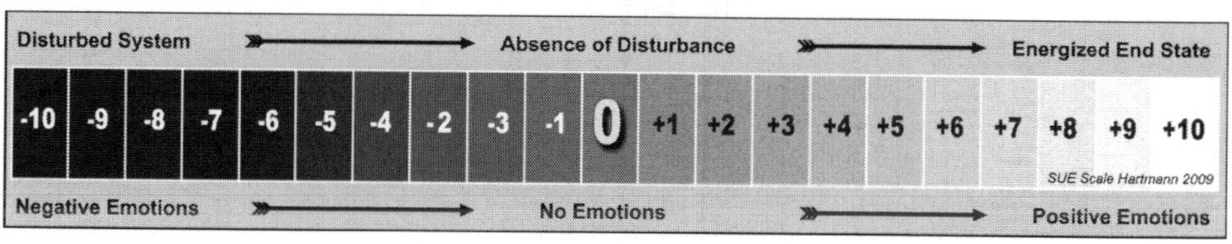

To simplify what The SUE Scale can help us with I would like you to imagine a ladder formed of 20 steps, this is making the assumption that the floor/ground are -10.

When we are at -10, we feel stuck, trapped, the energy has been sucked out of us and nothing makes sense. In fact, there is so much stress that is blinds us and everything seems incoherent.

Then we move on the first step, we are now at -9, we are still feeling stressed, we may get panic attacks, unconsciousness, yet everything still seems pointless.

In the following steps, the second, third, fourth, fifth and sixth; which would relate to -8 to -4 and believe it or not this is where many people are at in the world, this is where we have been brought to believe is a "good" place to be.

Take a look around you and you will see people with very high levels of stress to medium levels of stress, and you will hear them saying things like: it is life! If you don't run like a headless chicken you aren't doing much. Their thoughts and behaviours are erratic and out of control.

Then we have the seventh, eighth and ninth steps, these relate to -3 to -1. Here life starts getting better, people are starting to even consider the idea of dreaming again, that there may be hope after all and the stress levels are lower.

The tenth step, relates to 0. Here there is no stress, we feel calm, tranquil and restful. Though we aren't living to our full potential. Life is good (according to people's views) and we may still be afraid to cross the fence and experience life on the + side.

So, now we are on the + side…

I promise you, life does get a lot better, sweeter, greater, more fun and exciting when we cross this side of the "stress fence"…

The eleventh step is +1. Here for the first time many people will start experiencing energy flow, it may be slow at first but it is much better than what you experience on the – side. You feel neutral about life, you start developing your awareness and you start feeling positive thoughts and emotions.

As I write on The SUE Scale and now that I am writing about the + side of the scale I can feel my own Energy levels raising and energising me…

The twelfth step is +2. Again the energy flow is slow, but gradually increasing. At this level is like "waking up from a deep sleep".

The thirteenth step is +3. The energy levels at this level are medium, and for the first time many people experience a sense of wellness, feeling OK, enjoying and living the present and self-worth.

The fourteenth step is +4. Here the energy continues to improve and its flow increases, we feel an increased body awareness, we feel good and start thinking of the future (maybe even for the first time in our lives!).

The fifteenth step corresponds to +5. The energy continues to improve and increase, we start feeling wide awake, happy and ready for action. We start feeling hopeful and unstoppable.

At this point I would like to highlight that those who experience the + side of The SUE Scale sometimes don't get past +5.

This could be for various reasons, the environment, unhealed wounds from the past, or Stress slowly creeping up into their lives…

It continues to get better…

The next step correlates to +6. There is a faster energy flow, we feel powerful and excited.

Then…

At +7 (step seventeenth), there is a very fast flow of energy, again we feel powerful and mostly our emotions are positive ones.

In the eighteenth step, at +8. There is a uniquely high energy flow, we start experiencing fast and logical thinking, as well as high rapport and communication with others.

At +9, there is a very high energy flow. We can't help but to feel delighted, very excited and joyful, there aren't many reasons as to why we shouldn't be feeling this way at this level.

And…

Finally, the twentieth step, +10.

This is who we truly are!

The energy flows the way is meant to do, optimally. We are truly enlightened, everything, absolutely everything we are, do and have at this level is the way is meant to be.

We feel and live true and unconditional love.

At +10 there is no time for nothing else but love and happiness. When we are in our rightful place, everything falls into place and there is no room for anything else.

Now, I invite you to go up that imaginary ladder in your mind's eye.

Start on the ground at -10, where nothing makes sense and confusion reigns.

Take your time to feel the energy at each one of the different levels, and shake it all off when you come out of it, before you move on the next one.

I encourage you to take a good while at 0, where calmness and tranquillity rule, yet there is no hope or an overall passion for life and love.

As before, shake it all off before you move onto the + side.

When you end at the top of the ladder (it could literally be the top of the world!), experience yourself and energy levels at this level.

What does it feel like? What are you feeling in your body? Would you like more of it?

Lastly, I would like you remember you are in control of your thoughts and energy, so whenever you are feeling low in energy or stressed, remember The SUE Scale and take yourself to the + side, all the way to +10 and stay there … It is your birthright!

Heart Power Technique

The "Heart of Energy" is the power centre of the energy body.

- **Point to your chest with your leading hand to find your heart centre.**
- **Place the palm of your leading hand on that spot, then place the other hand on top.**
- **This is The Heart Position.**
- **Notice the sensations of your hands on your chest.**
- **Take three deep slow breaths, in and out.**

Something To Love

In the Heart Position, keep breathing and think of some one or somet hing you really love. Focus on how it makes you feel inside.

Breathe Out Stress, Breathe In Success

In the Heart Position, breathe out your stress on the out breath, and on the in breath, breathe in fresh air and energy.

Here & Now

In the Heart Position, breathe deeply. Note what you can see, hear, feel, scent, taste and how you feel inside (6th Sense).

Use the Heart Position at any time to stabilise yourself, to stop stress from escalating, and to raise energy.

The Heart Power is a very easy exercise.

Here is what you do:

1. Point to your chest with your dominant hand and find your heart centre.
2. Place the palm of the dominant hand on that spot, then place the other hand on top.
3. Pay attention and notice the sensations of your hands while on your heart area and position.
4. Take three deep and slow breaths, in and out.

These are some variations to the Heart Power Technique:

Find Something To Love

In the heart position, keep breathing and think of someone or something you really love. Focus on how it makes you feel inside.

Breathe Out Stress, Breathe In Success

In the heart position, in the out breath, breathe out your stress and in the in breath, breathe in fresh air, energy and success. Repeat three times, or as many times as you feel it may be required.

Here and Now

In the heart position, breathe deeply. Note what you can see, hear, feel scent, taste and how you feel inside (your 6th sense).

Use the heart position at any time you need to "stabilise" yourself, to stop stress from escalating and to raise your energy.

Note: You can use The SUE Scale together with the Heart Power Technique. Firstly, check where you are at on The SUE Scale, choose the exercise you want or you feel will benefit you the most. When you are finished, check on the scale and see how far on the scale you have come to. Repeat as necessary.

With thanks to Silvia Hartmann,
from ***The Trillion Dollar Stress Solution***

Positive EFT

We go in life aimlessly and we tend to forget about the good things in life, and all its positives.

With Positive EFT you can (once again!), summon all of those positives you always wanted and still want just by tapping on yourself and summoning those positive attributes and qualities you want.

Good Energy With Positive EFT

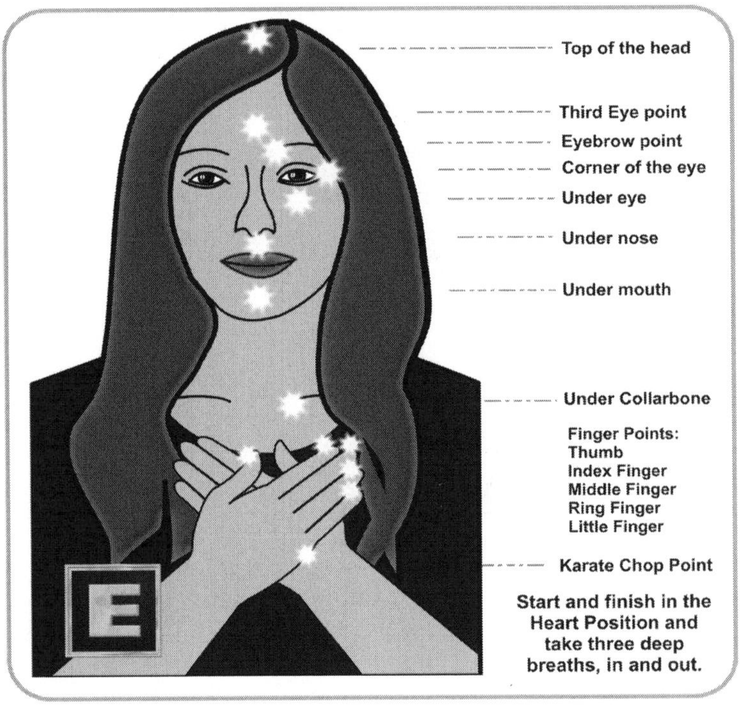

What would you like to have more of in your life?
Tap or simply touch all the points and say the word.

For a real energy boost, do all 9 - which one do you pick first ...?

Energy	Happiness	Success
Power	Love	Money
Vitality	Clarity	Confidence

First, decide what you would like more of… Is it Love? Energy? Patience? Success? Money? Confidence? Clarity? Wisdom?

The options and possibilities are endless…

Taking three deep breaths in and out on the heart position, focus your intention and energy on what is you want.

Then start tapping…

Let's do a tapping round on confidence.

- Place your hands on the heart position. Take three deep breaths in and out, and as you do this focus all your intention and energy on confidence, Growing Confident, being more confident.
- Tap lightly with your index finger on to the top of the head (still breathing in and out), and ask for more confidence. You can ask out loud or in silence, though saying it out loud feels better.
- Tap on to the third eye, say it again, I want to Grow Confident… And see it in your mind's eye, a confident you.
- Eyebrow point, more confidence… See through the eyes of a confident person.
- Corner of the eye, I am confident. Say it as loud as you can as you tap, I am confident.
- Under the eye, waking confidence in you. Being more confident.
- Under the nose, smelling the success of a confident person, even more confidence.
- Under the mouth, speaking like a confident person. I am confident.
- Under the collar bone, feeling confident. Even more confidence.
- Thumb, feeling even more confident, I am confident.
- Index finger, walking confidently, more confidence.
- Middle finger, I am Growing Confident. I am confident.
- Ring finger, I walk as a confident person, even more confidence.
- Little finger, I am confident and I will continue to be.
- Karate chop point, I am confident, I see, hear and feel like a confident person.

Then end your round with both hands back on the heart centre, feeling that confidence and energy raised in you.

Note: You can use The SUE Scale together with Positive EFT. Firstly, check where you are at on The SUE Scale, choose what you want more of or what you will benefit from the most. When you are finished, check on the scale and see how far on the scale you have come to. Repeat as necessary.

With thanks to Silvia Hartmann, from ***Positive EFT****.*

Take a Mini Holiday!

If you are like me, I am sure there has been a time when you wished you could have taken a Holiday to renew and revitalise you, and be as far away as possible from stressing places and situations.

Well, it pleases me to tell you that now you can!

It is really simple and it doesn't require much effort, only your imagination and two minutes…

Closing your eyes and placing your hands on your heart centre, say to your mind,

"Take me to the perfect place in time and space for me right not…"

- What is the time of the day?
- What is the time of the year?
- What is the weather?
- What is the landscape?
- What else is there?

How do you feel inside?

Make it even stronger…

- What can you see?
- What can you hear?
- What can you feel?
- What can you scent?
- What can you taste?

And…

- How does it make you feel inside?

Let these images and landscapes in your mind develop and take any learnings from it.

Remember, this is your mind communicating with you through metaphors and images.

Note: You can use The SUE Scale together with the Mini Holiday Technique. Firstly, check where you are at on The SUE Scale. When you are finished, check on the scale and see how far on the scale you have come to. Repeat as necessary.

With thanks to Silvia Hartmann,

from ***Infinite Creativity***.

About The Author

Jorge Vence was born in Panama City, Panama in 1983.

In the year 2000 Jorge, in his words "chose to be better", and he made the decision to add value to the lives of as many people as he could and so a journey began that ultimately led him to not only moved countries but continents too – to the UK.

Jorge now lives in Southampton, England were he has lived since December of 2002.

Like many people, Jorge knew he had a desire to help people but he just didn't know how. After almost 7 years in hospitality and retail Jorge, through study and experience, found his true passion in helping others in the area of Leadership and Management.

Jorge also trained to become a Life and Business Coach, EFT & NLP Master Practitioner & Trainer, Modern Stress Management Facilitator & Trainer, Reiki Master & Teacher and now an author and lecturer in what he teaches.

Jorge runs regular seminars, workshops, programmes and trainings in Southampton, Hampshire, and wishes to continue to share more hope through the written word.

Contact Jorge at

JorgeVence.com